U0486192

道本同揆
止止山房捐赠西泠印社域外印章集

All Truths Are One
Foreign Seals of Zhizhi Shanfang
Donated to Xiling Seal Engraver's Society

西泠印社 编
Edited by Xiling Seal Engraver's Society

何连海 主编
Chief Editor He Lianhai

阿克瑟斯文明卷
Oxus Civilization Volume

西泠印社出版社

道本同揆

止止山房捐赠西泠印社域外印章集
编委会

All Truths Are One

Foreign Seals of Zhizhi Shanfang Donated
to Xiling Seal Engraver's Society

Editorial Board

主　编	何连海	Chief Editor	He Lianhai
副主编	古　菲 / 吴佳玮 / 韩牧哲	Associate Editor	Gu Fei / Wu Jiawei / Han Muzhe
编　委	苏贻绪 / 郁　冰 / 许益友	Editorial Staff	Su Yixu / Yu Bing / Xu Yiyou
	赵俊然 / 杨謦闻 / 胡　琦		Zhao Junran / Yang Qingwen / Hu Qi
摄　影	张新民 / 姚智文	Photographer	Zhang Xinmin / Yao Zhiwen
装　帧	杨　宇	Book Designer	Yang Yu

关于域外印
《道本同揆 —— 止止山房捐赠西泠印社域外印章集》序

◎文 / 陈振濂

"域外印"是一个近两年才出现的概念。在几千年印学史和几百年篆刻史中，原本我们并没有这个概念。它是改革开放新时代以后孕育产生的新概念，还是二十一世纪二十年代以后，由当代印学史所新创的新概念。因为在古代，没有这一概念得以生长的土壤。

今天我们对它的认知背景，首先是基于日趋繁荣昌盛、与时俱进的百年名社西泠印社正在主张并实际倡导的"世界印章史"的宏大立场。

关于它的足迹，应该有如下的记录可按：

2016年，西泠印社策划了第一个涉及域外印内容的图形印与非汉字系统印章国际印学研讨会并出版论文集。

2018年，西泠印社再一次主办了与域外印直接相关联的世界图纹与印记国际学术研讨会也出版了论文集。

2019年，相关几位同仁开始策划"一带一路"图形印主题范围的创作实践项目。操作方案已完成，后因新冠肺炎疫情而搁置。三年后的2022年才重新启动，成立了"一带一路·图形印"的专题创作科研实验组，并在第一批科研创作成果推出以后，开始尝试在全国范围推进图形印作品的征稿公募，由此，篆刻性质的创作实践探索科研活动，从无到有，在业界获得了充分展开的机会。每年一届，今年已是第三届了；经过三年积累，它已经成为当代印学史上一个引人注目的亮点，受到越来越广泛的关注。

从学术概念梳理层面上看，域外印并不是在一开始就被大家所认可的。中国古代与近代印学史、篆刻史的思想建设和观念生长，一向有长期偏向于内省自足而没有机会向外看的习惯——篆刻肯定是传统文化，是国粹，是老祖宗留传下来的宝贝，必须不折不扣地被我们这一代奉行之，坚守之，沿循之。在美术界，多有受西方世界影响投射，甚至不断出现用现代艺术改造中国画而且成功的案例；但书法界则因为西方本没有书法这一门类，所以总体上并没有遭受太明显的西方影响。即使有极少部分书法界人士一意孤行奉行西方主义，但其实践结果一公布于世，必会引起轩然大波导致纷争攻讦，闹得不可开交。从二十世纪八十年代中期到二十一世纪二十年代的当下，这三十年间的头尾两段时间，在社会舆情和同行评论领域中，尤其表现激烈而毫不留情。相比之下，篆刻界却是一直保持事不关己、漠不关心的态度，平静寂寞，波澜不惊；但同时也明显表现出缺乏广博的世界眼光和缺少丰富想象力未能勇于开拓的尴尬状态。与各门类艺术如音、舞、剧、画、塑、影、视等，可以说是完全不同频而只能孤独前行。

于是，我们今天来看域外印的定位，除了努力继承图形印、"世界图纹印记"已有的创新概念之外，又必须具有不尽相同而又更进一步、更开阔的世界史眼光。

比如图形印概念，它是针对传统篆刻的文字印（古文字篆书印）的源远流长而发，其关系是文与图的关系；它关注的，是字形和图形的视觉差异问题，而不必涉及中华文明与西方文明、中国与外国以及由此而来的区域、民族、宗教的关系。

但域外印的定义，却牵涉到国家与国家，区域与区域，文明形态与文明形态甚至宗教、民族、历史、文化符号象征的诸多要素。它不仅仅是图形的视觉差异问题，它还是人文与历史、民族的文化差异问题，因此需要更多的知识储备与见多识广的价值观、世界观的支撑。而这对于像篆刻艺术这样比较内向内省的偏古代的传统艺术门类而言，其挑战尤其严峻，甚至也许还会让人感觉似乎是更难以胜任、遥不可及。

西泠印社正是在这样的时代背景、历史背景和专业背景之下，审时度势，积极主动接受挑战。平心而论，其实并没有人从外部客观环境对我们提出要求或作出过明确的指令、催促、规定。但我们认为站在"文化自信""中国文化走出去"的国家立场上看篆刻艺术，我们这些印学中人应该有这样自觉的责任心、使命感。从2016年开始策划启动围绕篆刻图形印的新研究，提倡立足专业，放眼世界，以占据学理上的先鞭，复能在古典印学史上"为王前驱"。而且为了避免盲目冲动而坠入肤浅庸俗，西泠印社组织召开了2016年、2018年两次国际学术研讨会，理清脉络，疏浚思维。有了相应充分的学术理论准备，才开启创作实践层面上作为面向新未来新发展的措施和部署。

但要进行这样一个新时代印学史的"新长征"，要充分汲取贯穿古代几千年延续至今的、寄托于印章篆刻的金石美学传统（当然汉代即已有肖形印、图形印传统，只是规模数量很少），以之作为今天推动图形印和域外印的审美定位和出发点，自然是必须的、毋庸置疑的。而作为域外印的形制、形式与视觉图像等来自他国他域的异质传统，由于多年的闭关锁国和专业视线的封闭狭窄原因，举目望去，我们过去百年间在这方面几乎没有积累（当然也没有条件积累）。如果不是改革开放四十年依托国门开放所带来的逐渐扩大的世界视野，国际交流条件也相应获得了大改善；如果还是困难重重到处都是认知障碍与操作瓶颈，我相信篆刻界仍然不会有我们所期望的积极反应与配合甚至投入。那么已有的三届"一带一路·图形印展"即"印·世界""文明互鉴"和2025年"世界图纹印记"的全国性图形印大展的征稿评选和展览，就肯定推动不起来。但现在，应者云集，热火朝天，证明群众基础在不断扩大并厚实，专业上已成气候，社会公众的认知度处于十分理想的状态。

正是在这个节点上，何连海社兄的域外印捐赠，已经或将来必然会起到一个非常重要的作用。

域外印的收集珍藏，机缘很少，不易实施。欧美的部分还好些；因为近四十年改革开放，我们的交流对象大半锚定欧美的发达国家，赴彼国的往返或留住的机会较多。而域外印的分布，古代至近世大部分在东亚、南亚、西亚和中东地区。从古代的萨珊波斯王朝、中亚希腊巴克特里亚、中东亚述、南亚贵霜，横贯两河流域的叙利亚、伊拉克、埃及直到地中海中部沿岸，再到今天的印度、巴基斯坦、阿富汗、南亚遗存、伊朗、土耳其直到中东阿拉伯的遗存。图形印、域外印涉及了古埃及文明、两河文明、希腊文明、印度文明，足以在域外领地充分撷取印章这一物质载体的层面上，而能与我们华夏文明毫无愧色地并驾齐驱。只不过，我们华夏文明有智慧有机遇，更把实用的印章转换成篆刻艺术，这是其他文明所没有的独特贡献。但反过来也证明了：域外印作为一个概念，这对我们专业的篆刻家而言，应该还是一个全新的存在。它的知识背景，是我们过去很陌生的世界印章史范围。

这批域外印作为"物"的价值，可以从材料、形制、内容三方面来作评估：

材料有滑石烧结、绿泥石、大理石、陶、铜、铁。

形制有印台印钮体状；有长、扁、棱、圆、楕、三角、边条各种印面形式。

内容有动物、植物、昆虫，属于纯粹的绘画式图形印。也有不写实而是装饰的图案纹样印：如回纹、水纹、树叶纹、各种几何纹、隔珠纹图案；更有图形加铭文字母，一般是"图"主"铭"次，"图"大"铭"小，有如汉印中的四灵印之类。

何连海社兄的域外印慷慨捐赠之壮举的另一个重要意义，是有效地填补了百年名社西泠印社专业收藏的空白。百年名社在早期收藏中，创社四子、吴昌硕和马衡以下一直到张鲁庵，后继的王福庵、王个簃、吴长邺诸先贤，在不同历史时期，都有大批量的各种珍贵文物捐献。百年社庆后，此一优良传统仍然"弦歌不辍"，全社上下捐赠之风益炽。但这次600余方域外印捐赠，却仍然引起了我们的高度重视。因为除古玺印捐赠、明清流派印与民国时期名家书画印的成批捐赠，又如社史中属于里程碑式的张鲁庵的四百多部古印谱捐赠之外，很少有人会去了解并去顾及域外还有印章。记得2016年的图形印与非汉字系统印章国际学术研讨会上，曾经还有专家认定印章的发明必然就是中国的，质疑连我们自己都不认老祖宗了？甚至指责这牵涉到爱国主义的问题；却全然不顾西亚中东和南亚的印章（包括青铜器）考古发掘证明时间上早于中国的历史事实。它表明，域外印还是一个"冷门绝学"式的空白地带，许多常识还未被普遍建立起来。

如果没有近三年推动"一带一路·图形印"的创作实践和2016年开始的国际学术研讨会理论研究，我们过去完全没有也不会去关注到这方面的信息。但当我们开始关注世界印章史并以"文明互鉴——一带一路·图形印"全国性篆刻印章创作实践进行展开之时，域外图形资料和文献的匮乏，成为我们的一个绕不过去的瓶颈。何连海社兄的捐赠，正好解决了我们推进图形印、域外印缺少参照物的难题，此举可谓是"及时雨"。如果假以时日，在今天比重占稍高的已有中亚、南亚诸品之外，在西亚中东部以现在为基础再继续增加，从而逐渐形成完整的庞大规模体系，则可以使百年西泠的印学收藏，再也没有明显的盲点。今后在印学创作实践与理论研究的任何一个方面，都能有效地积蓄力量，从而真正实现印学收藏"大印学"的壮观局面。

2025年1月15日于西泠印社

目 录
Contents

001 — 261　阿克瑟斯文明卷
　　　　　Oxus Civilization Volume

263 — 275　索引表
　　　　　Index

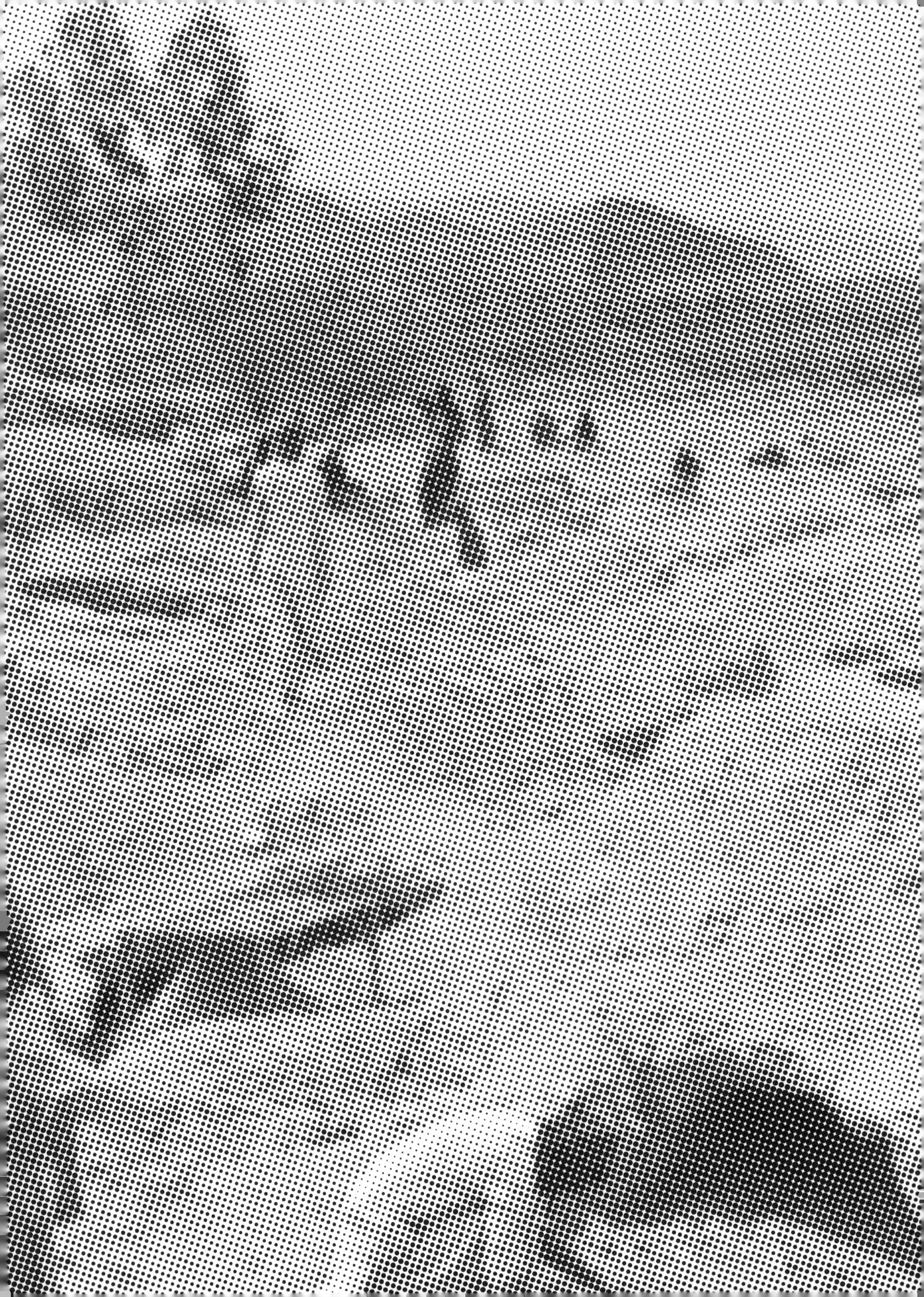

阿克瑟斯文明卷
Oxus Civilization Volume

阿克瑟斯文明

阿克瑟斯文明（Oxus Civilization）又称巴克特里亚－马尔吉亚纳考古共同体（Bactria-Margiana Archaeological Complex, BMAC），或青铜时代巴克特里亚（Bronze Age of Bactria），是青铜时代中亚地区文明的统称。这一文明区域以阿姆河为中心，包含阿富汗北部、伊朗东北部、乌兹别克斯坦南部、塔吉克斯坦西部和土库曼斯坦大部分区域。这些区域青铜时代的物质文化层面表现出一定的相似性和关联性，因此在1976年被苏联考古学家维克多·萨瑞阿尼迪（Viktor I. Sarianidi）笼统定名为BMAC。但从文明的中心性出发，当前历史学界更倾向于采用法国考古学家H. P. 法兰克福（Henri-Paul Francfort）提出的阿克瑟斯文明或阿姆河文明来指代。

阿克瑟斯文明自9200年前的新石器时代开始经历了持续的演化过程。虽然未发现文字，但公元前2000年左右开始出现了高度发达的城市文明。在这里的托格洛克（Togolok）、古诺尔（Gonur）、达施里（Dashli）、法罗尔（Fullol）丘地等遗址发现的大量精美珍贵的文物为我们展现了当年阿克瑟斯文明的繁荣。

阿克瑟斯文明与伊朗高原的原埃兰和吉罗夫特文明、两河文明及南部的印度河谷文明均有着非常密切的关联。在一定时期内，这里极有可能充当着连通印度河谷文明与两河文明的陆桥。阿克瑟斯文明的装饰品与同时期印度河谷文明有着极高的相似性，但在印章的制作和使用上独具特色。

阿克瑟斯文明的印章多使用青铜和当地常见的材料制作，如绿泥石、雪花石膏、叶腊石、青金石等。他们也使用烧结滑石制作吊坠和护身符一类的装饰品，但较少用它制作印章。此外，阿克瑟斯文明的印章通常是形制各异的平印，青铜印常采用镂空技法，造型也更为活泼，边缘可能采用花边、肖形等灵活形态。印章的题材多为神话中的人物或抽象的动物，以及高度抽象的几何图案、花纹与符号，尺寸通常悬殊。同一时期的遗址中既可能见到直径超过10厘米的大型印章，也可能见到印面厘米见方的小型印章。这些青铜印早期可能会在灼烧后烙印在牲畜及皮革上作为属权标志，后期则可能更多起到护身符的功用，也可能在陶器或封泥上作为装饰性印花工具使用。阿克瑟斯文明的印章上可见到一些影响深远的文化母题，例如两河文明神话与希腊神话中的"兽主"题材、战争与繁殖女神伊南娜、象征萨满教天地对立的鹰蛇搏斗题材。在青铜时代晚期，这些文化意象也有可能通过北方草原的游牧民族经由东北亚传至我国，对于我国早期的青铜玺印形态及部分区域性的图像印或许曾产生一定影响。

阿克瑟斯文明在青铜时代之后依然存续了不短的时间，其部分分支可能在公元前500年左右仍有存续，直至其先后被斯基泰人、波斯人统治、融合和分散。公元前四世纪亚历山大大帝率马其顿军团东征，将中亚地区收入囊中。亚历山大死后，其部将建立的塞琉古王朝在中亚地区设立边境总督，阿富汗一带也因此成为希腊人口中的"巴克特里亚"，并在公元前256年建立了希腊人主导的巴克特里亚王国。后来，巴克特里亚王国被从新疆西迁的大月氏人覆灭，后者建立了地跨中亚、南亚的贵霜帝国，并承袭了中亚希腊化的艺术遗产，大名鼎鼎的"黄金之丘"宝藏就是这一时期的遗存。但此时的巴克特里亚与青铜时代的阿克瑟斯文明已经几乎没有什么承袭性的文化关联了。

Oxus Civilization

The Oxus Civilization, also known as the Bactria-Margiana Archaeological Complex (BMAC) or the Bronze Age of Bactria, is a collective term for the Bronze Age civilizations in Central Asia. Centered around the Amu Darya River, this region encompasses northern Afghanistan, northeastern Iran, southern Uzbekistan, western Tajikistan, and most of Turkmenistan. The material culture of these areas has similarities and correlations to a certain extent during the Bronze Age, hence prompting the Soviet archaeologist Viktor I. Sarianidi to broadly categorize them as BMAC in 1976. However, from the perspective of the centrality of civilizations, the current historical academia prefers to use the term Oxus Civilization or Amu Darya Civilization, as proposed by French archaeologist Henri-Paul Francfort, to refer to this civilization.

The Oxus Civilization had undergone a continuous evolution since the Neolithic Age, beginning 9200 years ago. Although no written records have been discovered, a highly developed urban civilization emerged around 2000 BCE. Numerous exquisite and precious artifacts found at ruins such as Togolok, Gonur, Dashli, and Fullol demonstrate the prosperity of the Oxus Civilization at that time.

The Oxus Civilization had close connections with the Elamite and Jiroft Civilizations on the Iranian Plateau, the Mesopotamian Civilization, and the Indus Valley Civilization in the south. For a certain period, it likely served as a land bridge connecting the Indus Valley Civilization with the Mesopotamian Civilization. The decorations of the Oxus Civilization share a great degree of similarity with those of the contemporaneous Indus River Valley Civilization, while it characterized unique approach to making and using seals.

Seals of Oxus Civilization were typically made of bronze and locally abundant materials such as chlorite, alabaster, pyrophyllite, and lapis lazuli. They also used fired steatite to produce decorations such as pendants and talismans, but unusually for seals. The seals of the Oxus Civilization were usually flat and varied in shape. Bronze seals often employed hollow-out techniques and featured lively designs. The edges might adopted flexible designs such as lace or resembling certain shape. The subjects usually depicted mythical figures or abstract animals, as well as highly abstract geometric patterns, blooms, and signs. There was usually a huge disparity in size, with both large seals exceeding 10 centimeters in diameter and small seals with square surface and side length of just a few centimeters found in the contemporaneous ruins. These bronze seals may be used as marks of property by branding livestock and leather after burning, and late they likely served more as talismans or decorative stamping tools for pottery or soft clay. The seals of the Oxus Civilization show some profound cultural subjects, such as the "beast-master" subject from Mesopotamian and Greek mythology, the goddess Inanna associated with warfare and fertility, and the struggle of eagle and serpent which symbolizing the opposition between air and earth in shamanism. In the Late Bronze Age, these cultural images may have been transmitted to China via nomadic herdsmen of the northern grasslands through Northeastern Asia, potentially influencing the early forms of bronze seals and some regional graphic seals in China.

The Oxus Civilization continued to exist for a considerable period after the Bronze Age, with some branches possibly still existing around 500 BCE until they were eventually ruled, integrated, and dispersed by the Scythians and Persians. In the 4th century BCE, Alexander the Great led the Macedonian army on an eastward expedition, bringing Central Asia under his control. After Alexander's death, his generals established the Seleucid Empire, which set up border governors in Central Asia. As a result, the region around Afghanistan became known as "Bactria" among the Greeks. In 256 BCE, a Greek-dominated Bactrian Kingdom was established. Subsequently, the Bactrian Kingdom was destroyed by the Yuezhi people migrating westward from Xinjiang, who established the Kushan Empire spanning Central Asia and South Asia and inherited the artistic legacy of Hellenistic Central Asia. The famous treasure of "Tillya Tepe" (Golden Hill) belongs to this period. However, at this point, Bactria had little cultural continuity with the Oxus Civilization in Bronze Age.

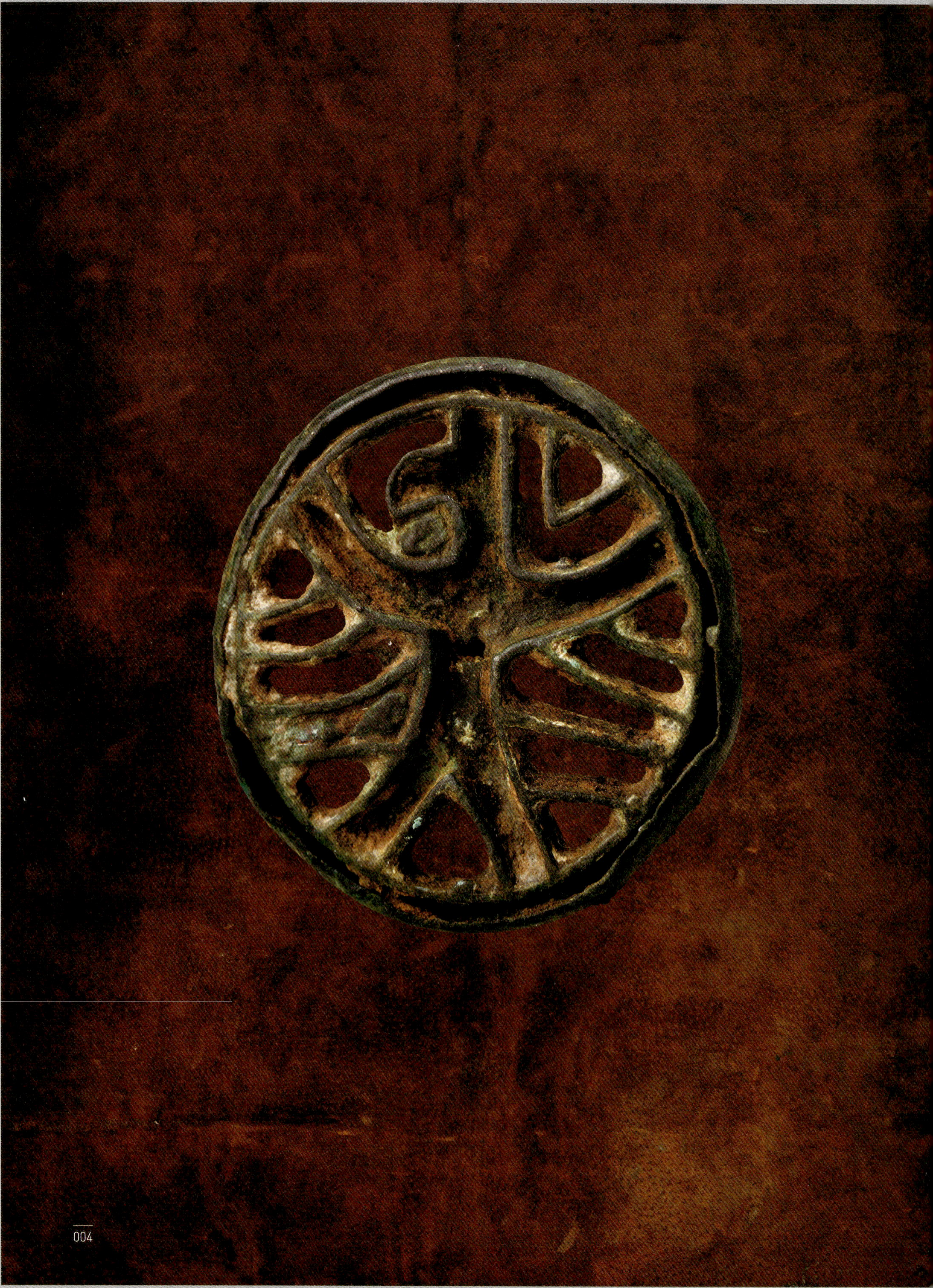

阿克瑟斯文明 Oxus Civilization

001

| 题材 Subject Matter |
| 人物 Humankind |

001

阿克瑟斯文明 Oxus Civilization   002   题材
Subject Matter

人物
Humankind

002

阿克瑟斯文明 Oxus Civilization

003

题材
Subject Matter

人物
Humankind

003

阿克瑟斯文明 Oxus Civilization　　004

| 题材
Subject Matter
| 人物
Humankind

004

阿克瑟斯文明　Oxus Civilization　　005　　| 题材
| Subject Matter
|
| 人物
| Humankind

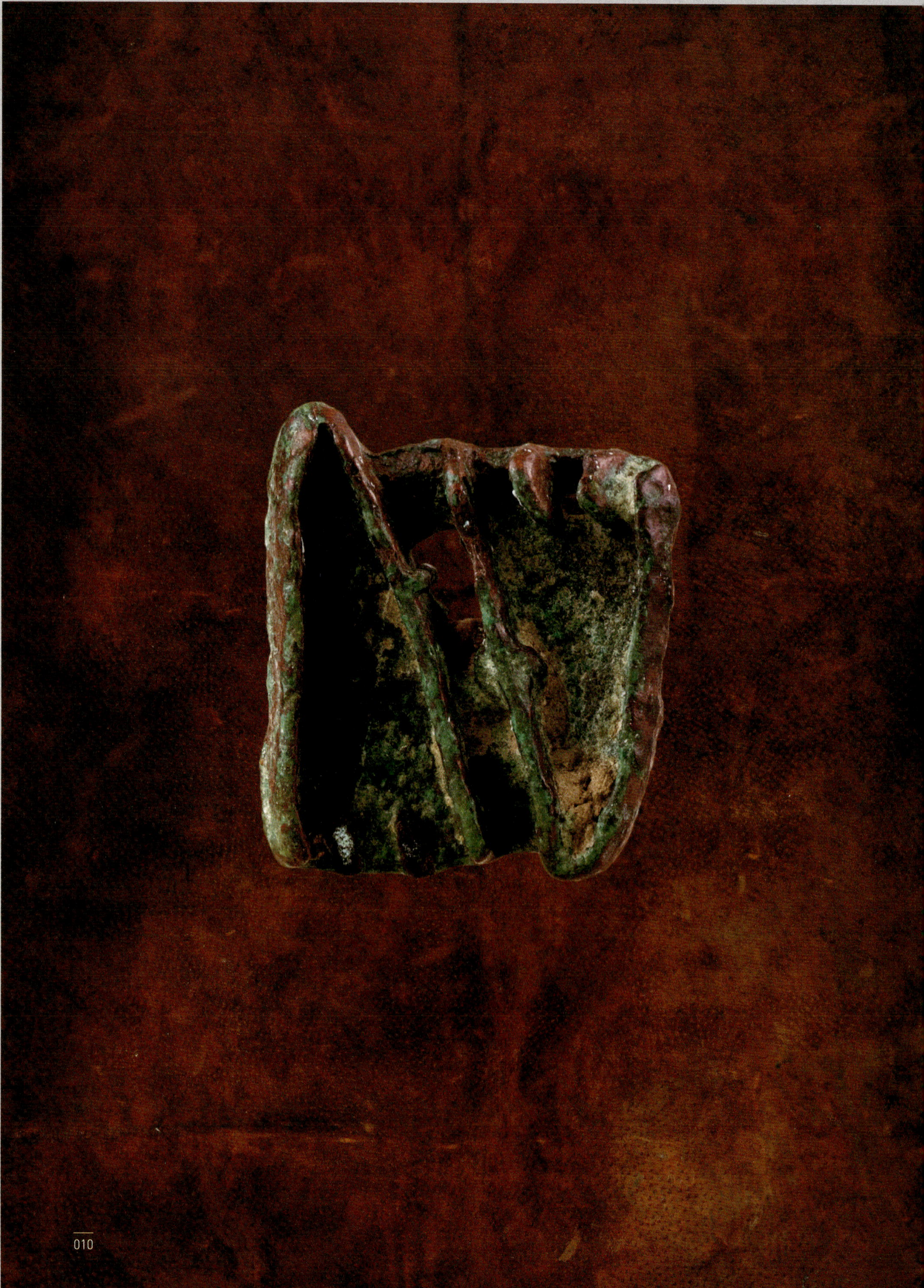

阿克瑟斯文明　Oxus Civilization	006	题材 Subject Matter
		人物（脚掌） Humankind (Sole)

006

阿克瑟斯文明　Oxus Civilization　　007-009

题材
Subject Matter

人物（脚掌）
Humankind (Sole)

007

008

009

阿克瑟斯文明 Oxus Civilization	010-012	题材 Subject Matter
		人物（脚掌） Humankind (Sole)

010

011

012

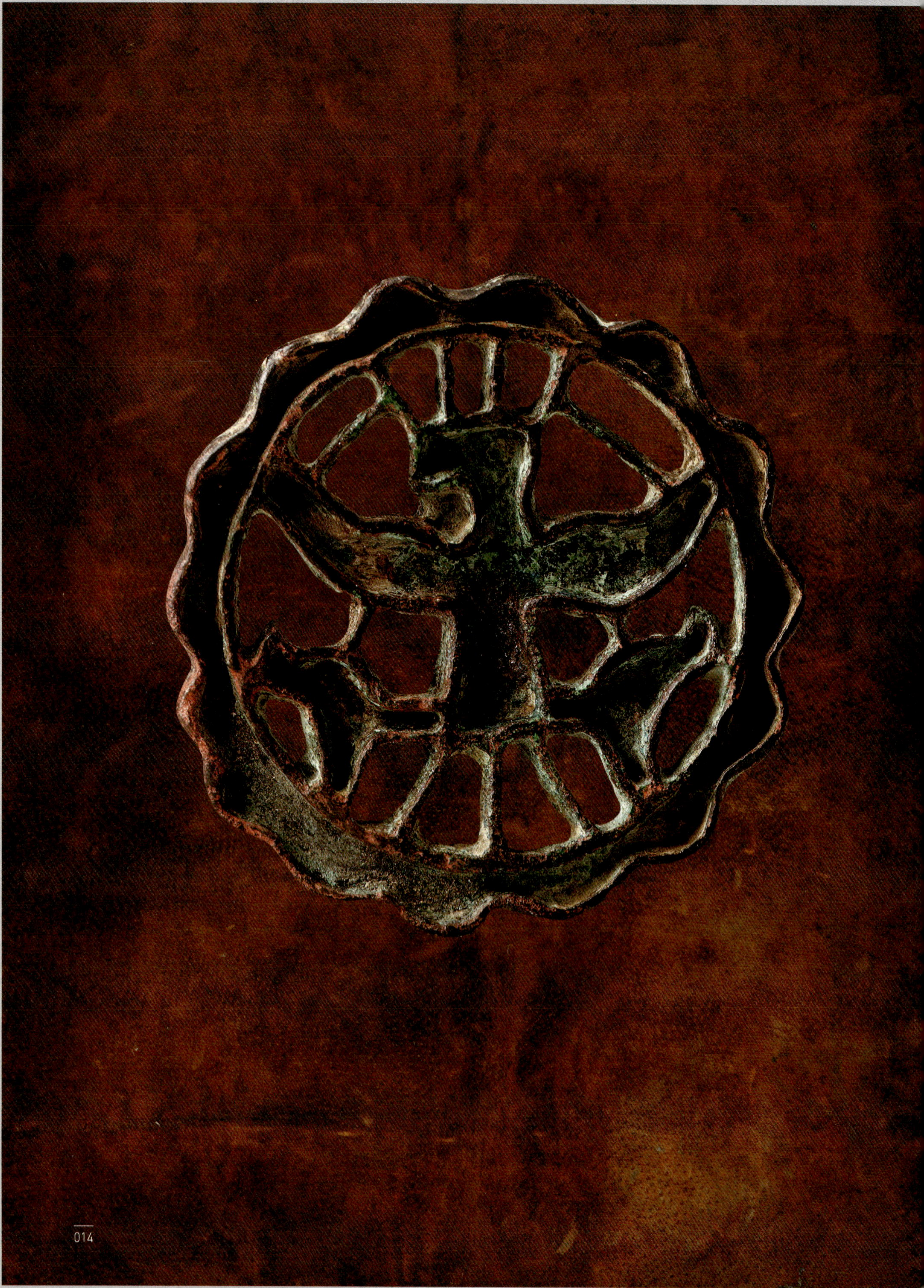

阿克瑟斯文明　Oxus Civilization　　013-014

题材
Subject Matter

动物
Animal

013

014

阿克瑟斯文明　Oxus Civilization　015-017　| 题材
| Subject Matter

| 动物
| Animal

015

016

017

阿克瑟斯文明　Oxus Civilization　018　| 题材
Subject Matter

| 动物
Animal

018

阿克瑟斯文明　Oxus Civilization　　019-021

题材
Subject Matter

动物
Animal

019

020

021

阿克瑟斯文明　Oxus Civilization

022

| 题材
Subject Matter

| 动物
Animal

022

| 阿克瑟斯文明　Oxus Civilization | 023-024 | 题材
Subject Matter |
| | | 动物
Animal |

023

024

阿克瑟斯文明 Oxus Civilization 025

题材 Subject Matter
动物 Animal

025

阿克瑟斯文明　Oxus Civilization　026　| 题材
| Subject Matter

| 动物
| Animal

026

阿克瑟斯文明 Oxus Civilization

027

| 题材 Subject Matter |
| 动物 Animal |

027

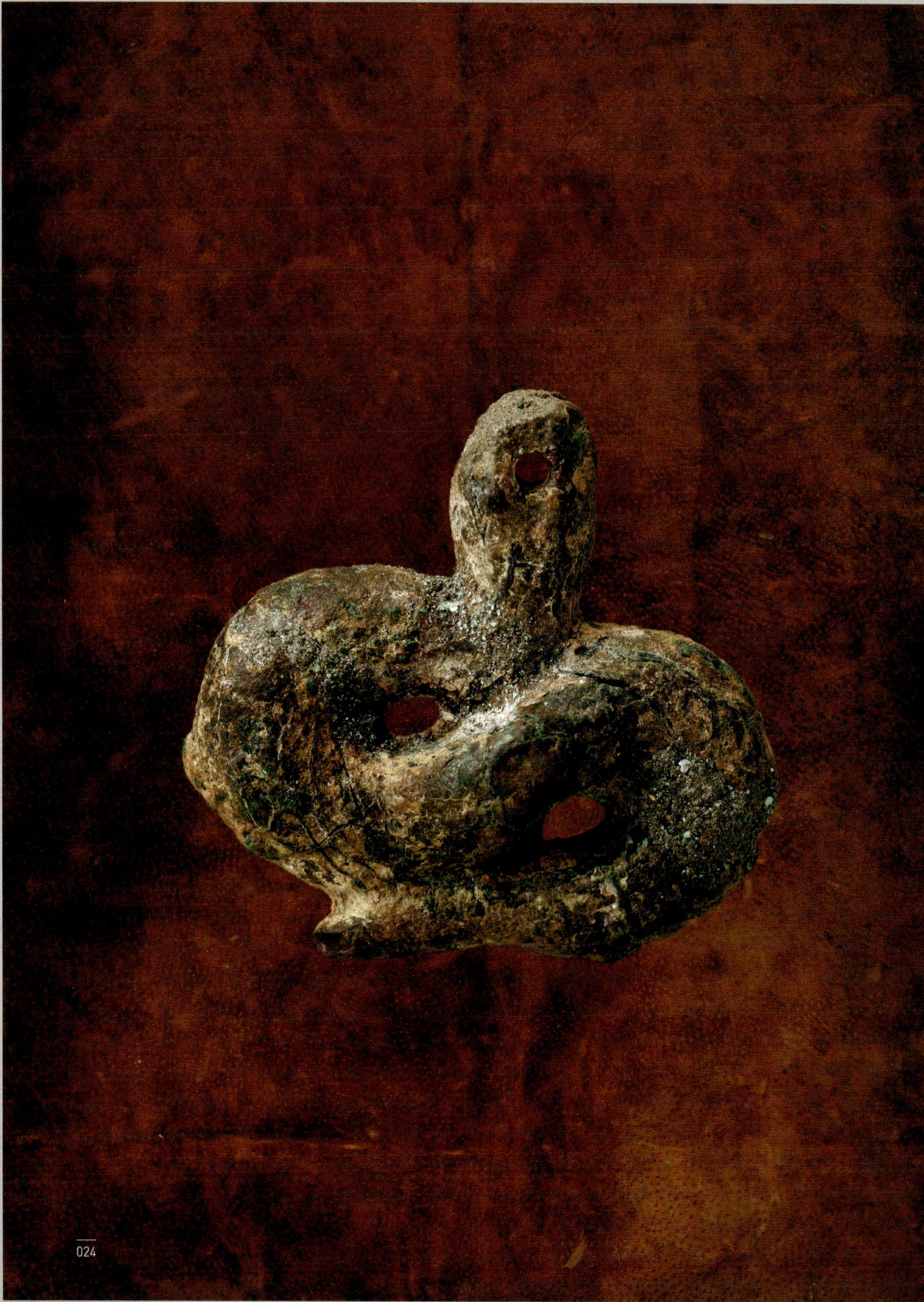

阿克瑟斯文明 Oxus Civilization 028

| 题材 Subject Matter |
| 动物 Animal |

028

阿克瑟斯文明　Oxus Civilization	029-030	题材 Subject Matter
		动物 Animal

029

030

阿克瑟斯文明 Oxus Civilization 031-032

题材
Subject Matter

动物
Animal

031

032

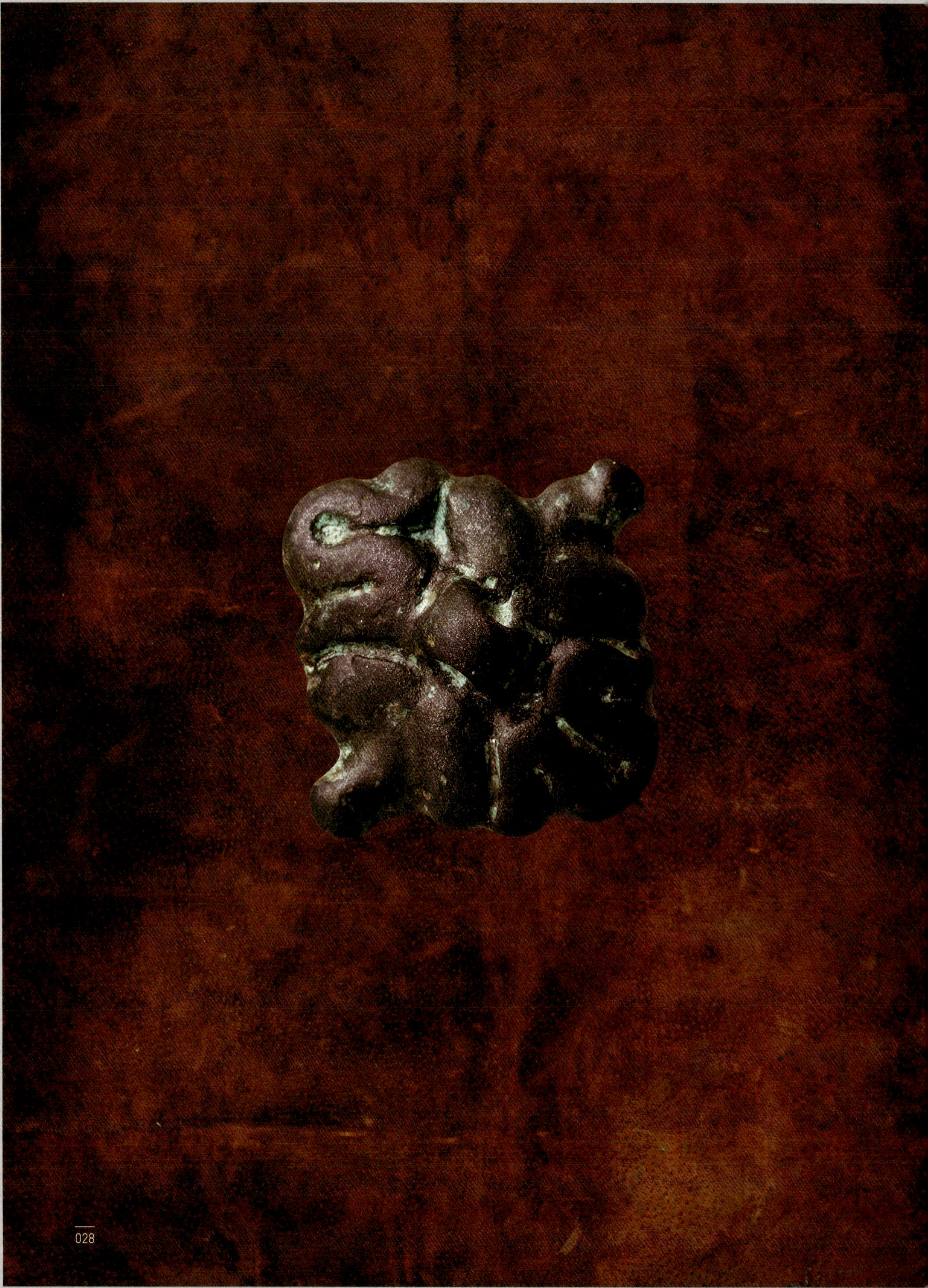

阿克瑟斯文明 Oxus Civilization

033

题材
Subject Matter

动物
Animal

| 阿克瑟斯文明 Oxus Civilization | 034 | 题材 Subject Matter |
| | | 动物 Animal |

034

阿克瑟斯文明 Oxus Civilization

题材
Subject Matter

动物
Animal

阿克瑟斯文明 Oxus Civilization　　036　　| 题材 Subject Matter
| 动物 Animal

036

阿克瑟斯文明　Oxus Civilization　　　037　　　| 题材
| Subject Matter

| 动物
| Animal

| 阿克瑟斯文明 Oxus Civilization | 038 | 题材 Subject Matter |
| | | 动物 Animal |

038

阿克瑟斯文明　Oxus Civilization　　039　　| 题材
| Subject Matter
| 动物
| Animal

039

阿克瑟斯文明 Oxus Civilization 040-041

题材
Subject Matter

动物
Animal

040

041

阿克瑟斯文明　Oxus Civilization 　042　　題材 Subject Matter / 动物 Animal

042

阿克瑟斯文明 Oxus Civilization	043-044	题材 Subject Matter
		动物 Animal

043

044

039

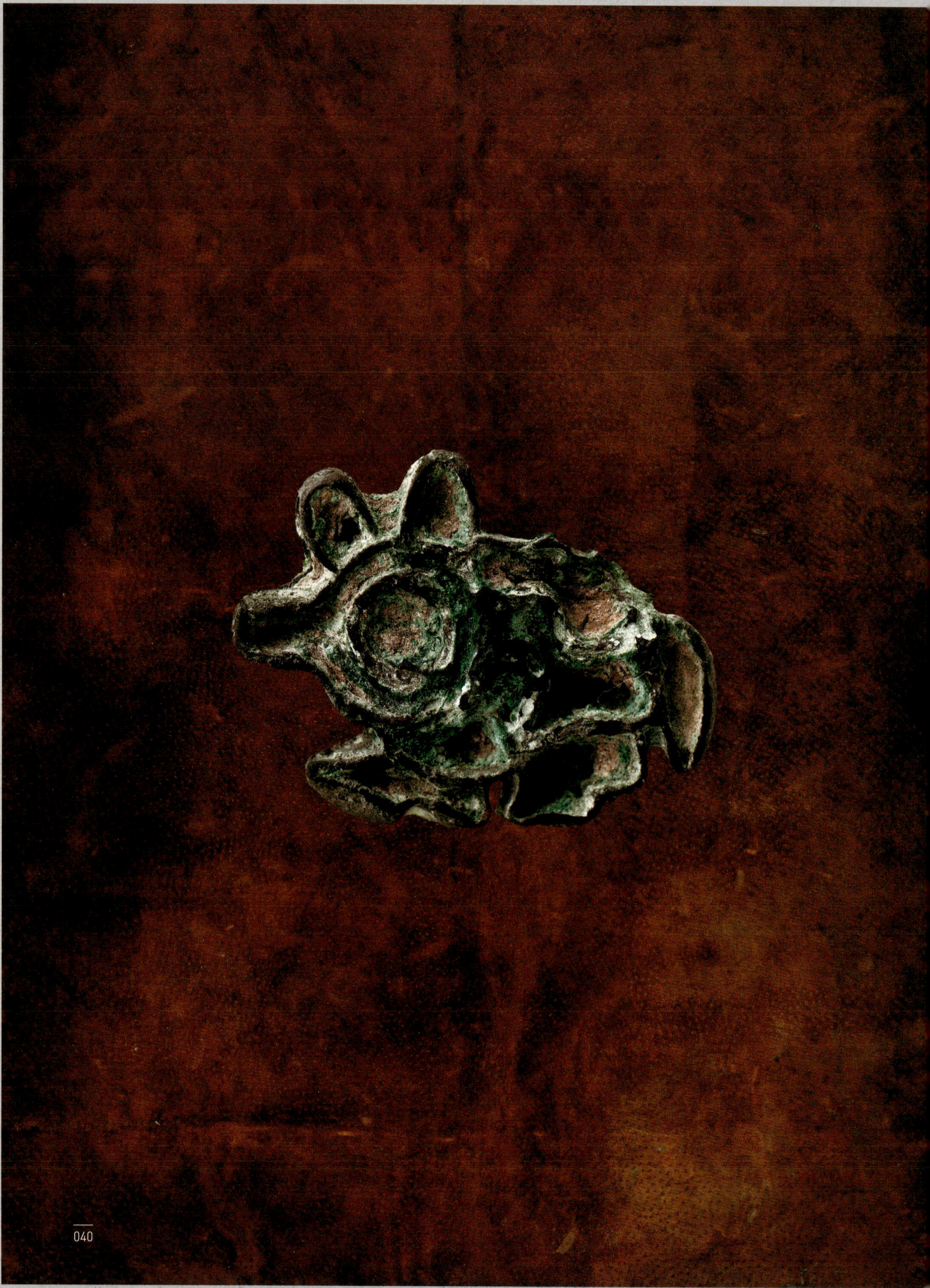

阿克瑟斯文明　Oxus Civilization　045

题材
Subject Matter

动物
Animal

045

阿克瑟斯文明　Oxus Civilization　046

题材
Subject Matter

动物
Animal

046

阿克瑟斯文明 Oxus Civilization 047

| 题材 Subject Matter |
| 动物 Animal |

047

阿克瑟斯文明 Oxus Civilization　048　题材 Subject Matter

动物 Animal

048

阿克瑟斯文明 Oxus Civilization   049-050

| 题材
| Subject Matter
|
| 动物
| Animal

049

050

045

阿克瑟斯文明 Oxus Civilization 051

题材
Subject Matter

动物
Animal

051

阿克瑟斯文明 Oxus Civilization

052

题材 Subject Matter
动物 Animal

052

阿克瑟斯文明 Oxus Civilization   053-054   题材
Subject Matter

动物
Animal

053

054

| 阿克瑟斯文明　Oxus Civilization | 055-056 | 题材　Subject Matter |
| | | 动物　Animal |

055

056

| 阿克瑟斯文明 Oxus Civilization | 057 | 题材 Subject Matter |
| | | 动物 Animal |

057

阿克瑟斯文明 Oxus Civilization 058-060

题材
Subject Matter

动物
Animal

058

059

060

| 阿克瑟斯文明 Oxus Civilization | 061-062 | 题材 Subject Matter |
| | | 动物 Animal |

061

062

052

阿克瑟斯文明 Oxus Civilization 063-064

| 题材 Subject Matter |
| 动物 Animal |

063

064

| 阿克瑟斯文明　Oxus Civilization | 065 | 题材　Subject Matter |
| | | 动物　Animal |

065

| 阿克瑟斯文明 Oxus Civilization | 066 | 题材 Subject Matter |
| | | 动物 Animal |

066

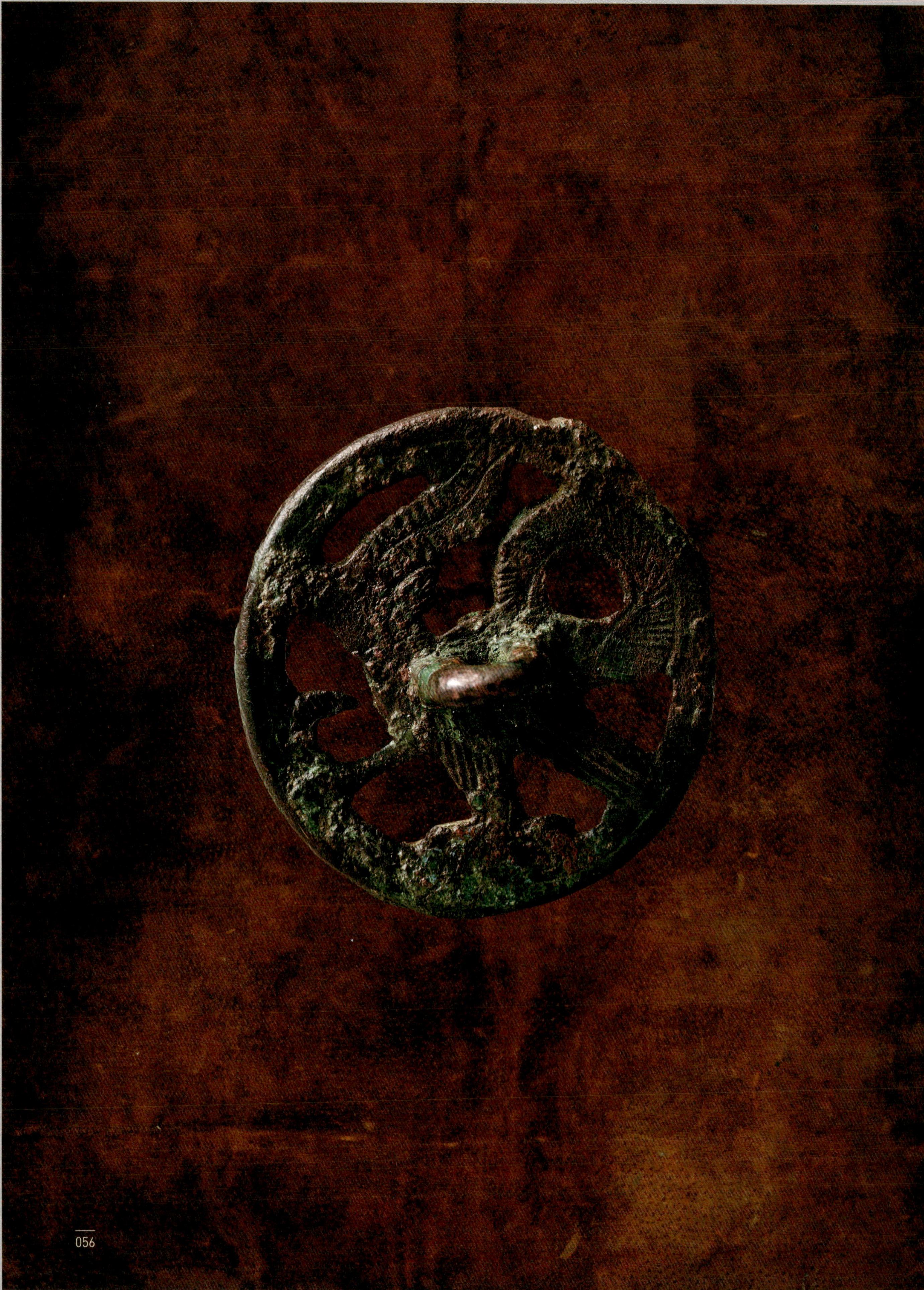

阿克瑟斯文明　Oxus Civilization

067

| 题材
| Subject Matter

| 动物
| Animal

067

阿克瑟斯文明 Oxus Civilization　　068　　题材 Subject Matter

动物 Animal

068

阿克瑟斯文明 Oxus Civilization 069

题材
Subject Matter

动物
Animal

069

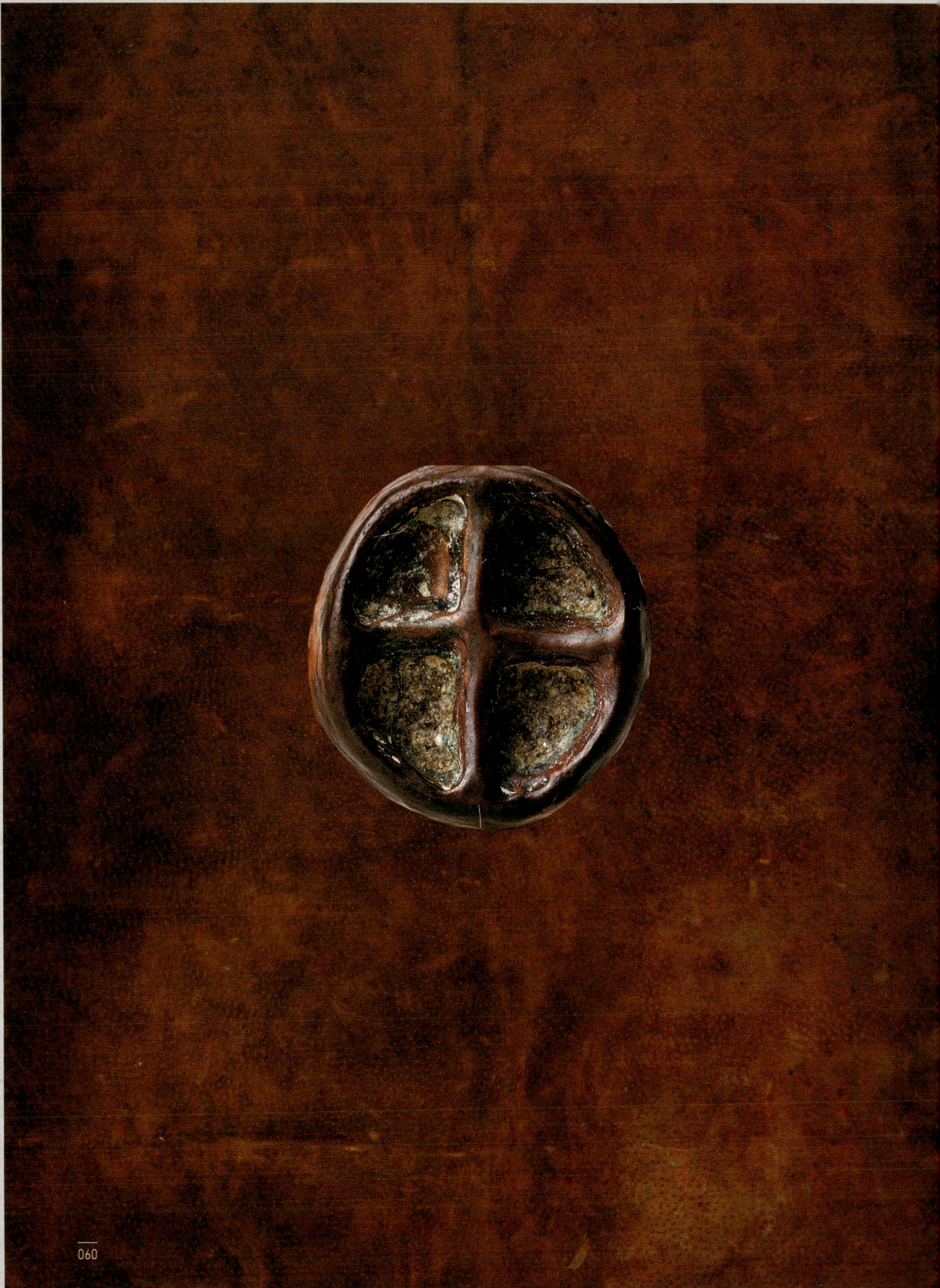

阿克瑟斯文明 Oxus Civilization   070-079

题材 / Subject Matter

几何纹 / Geometry Pattern

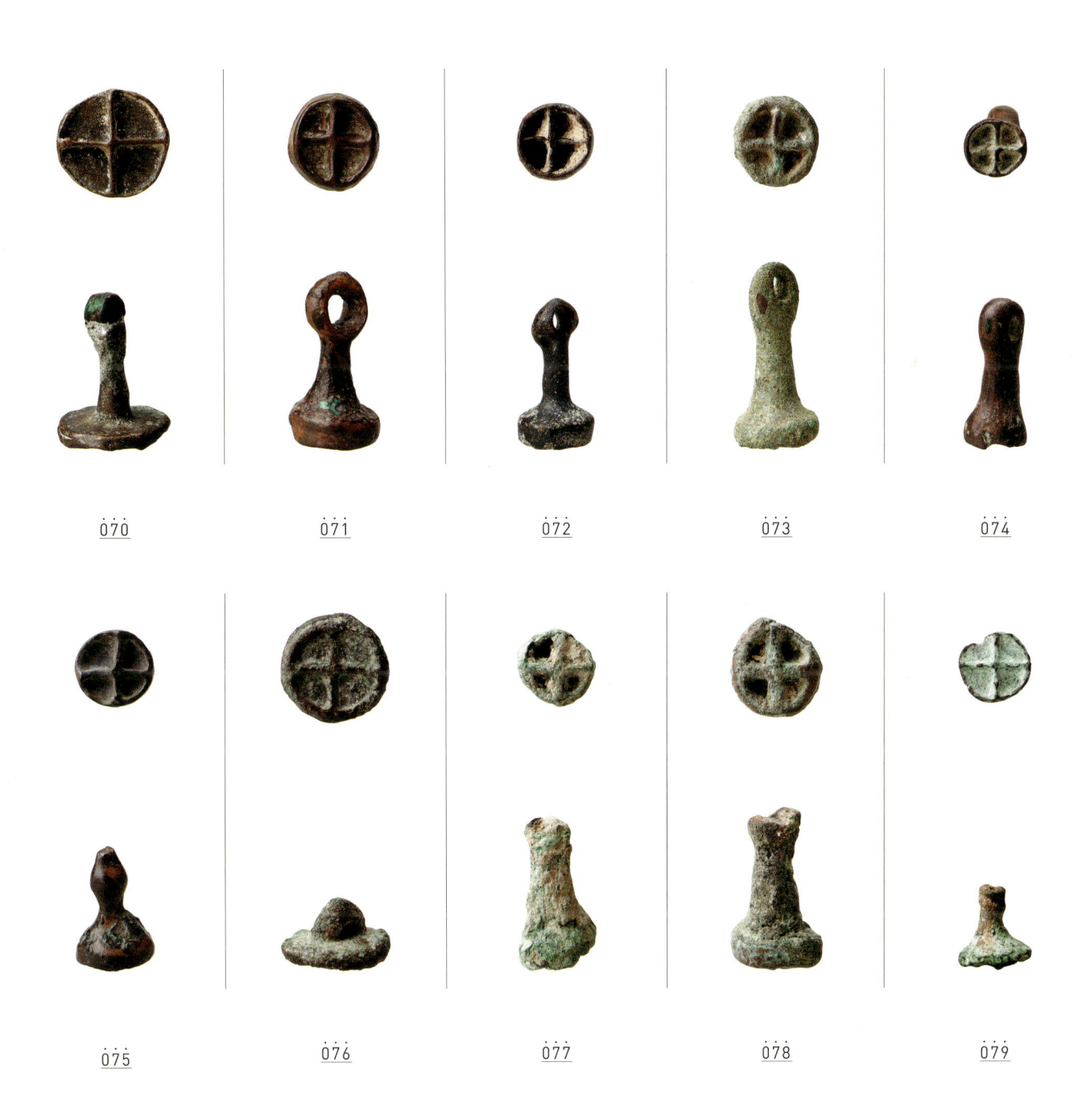

| 070 | 071 | 072 | 073 | 074 |

| 075 | 076 | 077 | 078 | 079 |

阿克瑟斯文明 Oxus Civilization   080-084

题材
Subject Matter

几何纹
Geometry Pattern

080   081   082   083   084

062

阿克瑟斯文明　Oxus Civilization　085-086

| 题材
Subject Matter

| 几何纹
Geometry Pattern

085

086

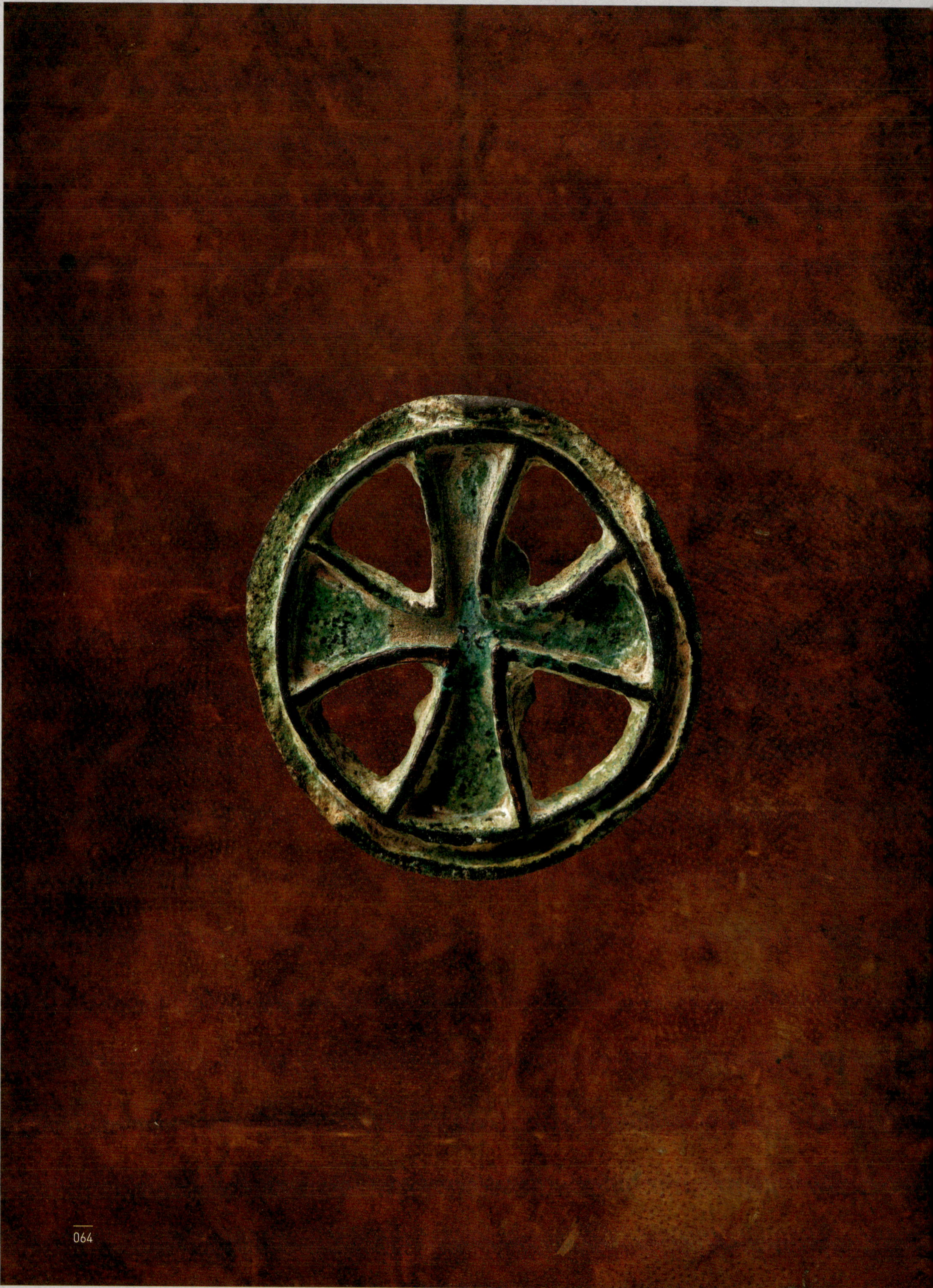

阿克瑟斯文明　Oxus Civilization　　087

题材
Subject Matter

几何纹
Geometry Pattern

087

| 阿克瑟斯文明 Oxus Civilization | 088-090 | 题材 Subject Matter |
| | | 几何纹 Geometry Pattern |

088

089

090

阿克瑟斯文明 Oxus Civilization 091-092

题材
Subject Matter

几何纹
Geometry Pattern

091

092

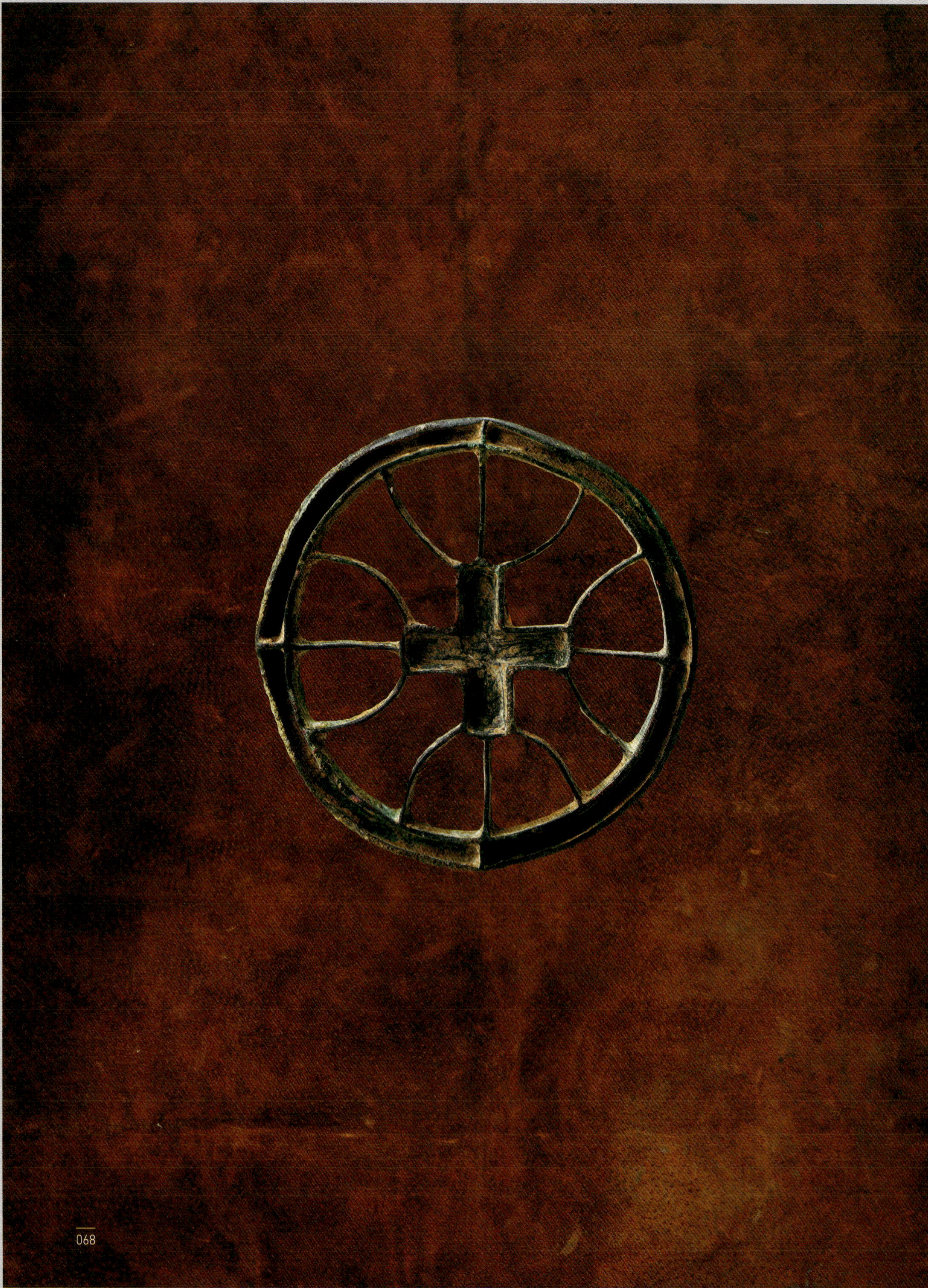

阿克瑟斯文明　Oxus Civilization　093

题材
Subject Matter

几何纹
Geometry Pattern

093

阿克瑟斯文明　Oxus Civilization　094

题材
Subject Matter

几何纹
Geometry Pattern

094

阿克瑟斯文明 Oxus Civilization　　095

题材　Subject Matter
几何纹　Geometry Pattern

095

阿克瑟斯文明 Oxus Civilization 096-097

题材
Subject Matter

几何纹
Geometry Pattern

096

097

阿克瑟斯文明 Oxus Civilization

098

题材
Subject Matter

几何纹
Geometry Pattern

098

阿克瑟斯文明 Oxus Civilization	099-100	题材 Subject Matter
		几何纹 Geometry Pattern

099

100

阿克瑟斯文明 Oxus Civilization

101

题材 Subject Matter
几何纹 Geometry Pattern

101

阿克瑟斯文明 Oxus Civilization

102

题材
Subject Matter

几何纹
Geometry Pattern

102

阿克瑟斯文明　Oxus Civilization　103-104

题材
Subject Matter

几何纹
Geometry Pattern

103

104

| 阿克瑟斯文明 Oxus Civilization | 105 | 题材 Subject Matter |
| | | 几何纹 Geometry Pattern |

105

阿克瑟斯文明 Oxus Civilization

106

题材
Subject Matter

几何纹
Geometry Pattern

106

阿克瑟斯文明 Oxus Civilization

107

题材
Subject Matter

几何纹
Geometry Pattern

107

阿克瑟斯文明　Oxus Civilization

108

题材 Subject Matter
几何纹 Geometry Pattern

108

| 阿克瑟斯文明　Oxus Civilization | 109 | 题材　Subject Matter |
| | | 几何纹　Geometry Pattern |

109

阿克瑟斯文明 Oxus Civilization

110

题材 Subject Matter
几何纹 Geometry Pattern

110

| 阿克瑟斯文明 Oxus Civilization | 111 | 题材 Subject Matter |
| | | 几何纹 Geometry Pattern |

111

084

阿克瑟斯文明　Oxus Civilization

112

题材
Subject Matter

几何纹
Geometry Pattern

112

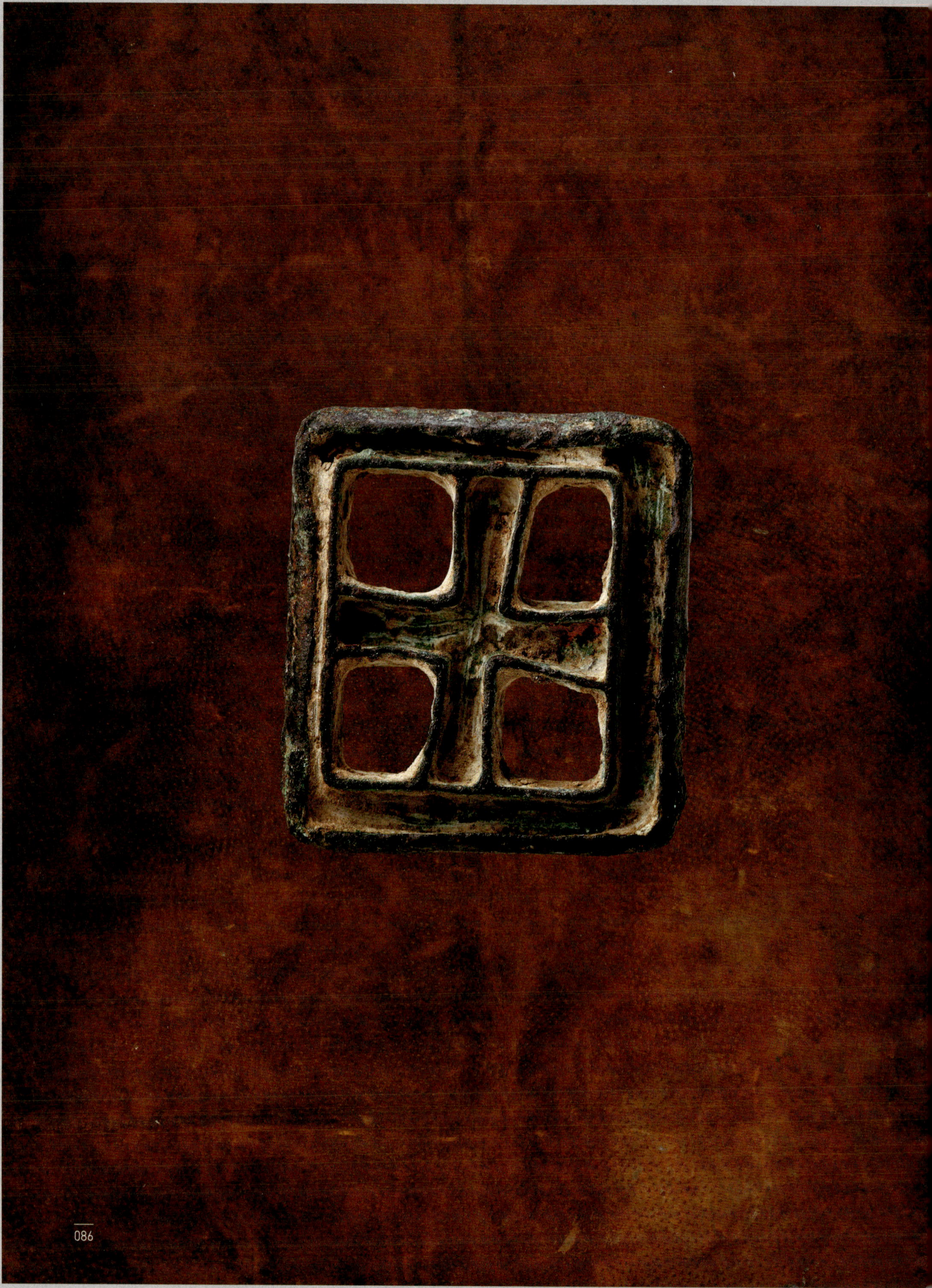

阿克瑟斯文明 Oxus Civilization 113

题材
Subject Matter

几何纹
Geometry Pattern

113

阿克瑟斯文明 Oxus Civilization   114-117

题材
Subject Matter

几何纹
Geometry Pattern

114   115   116   117

阿克瑟斯文明 Oxus Civilization | 118-120 | 题材 Subject Matter
| | 几何纹 Geometry Pattern

118　　　　　　　　　119　　　　　　　　　120

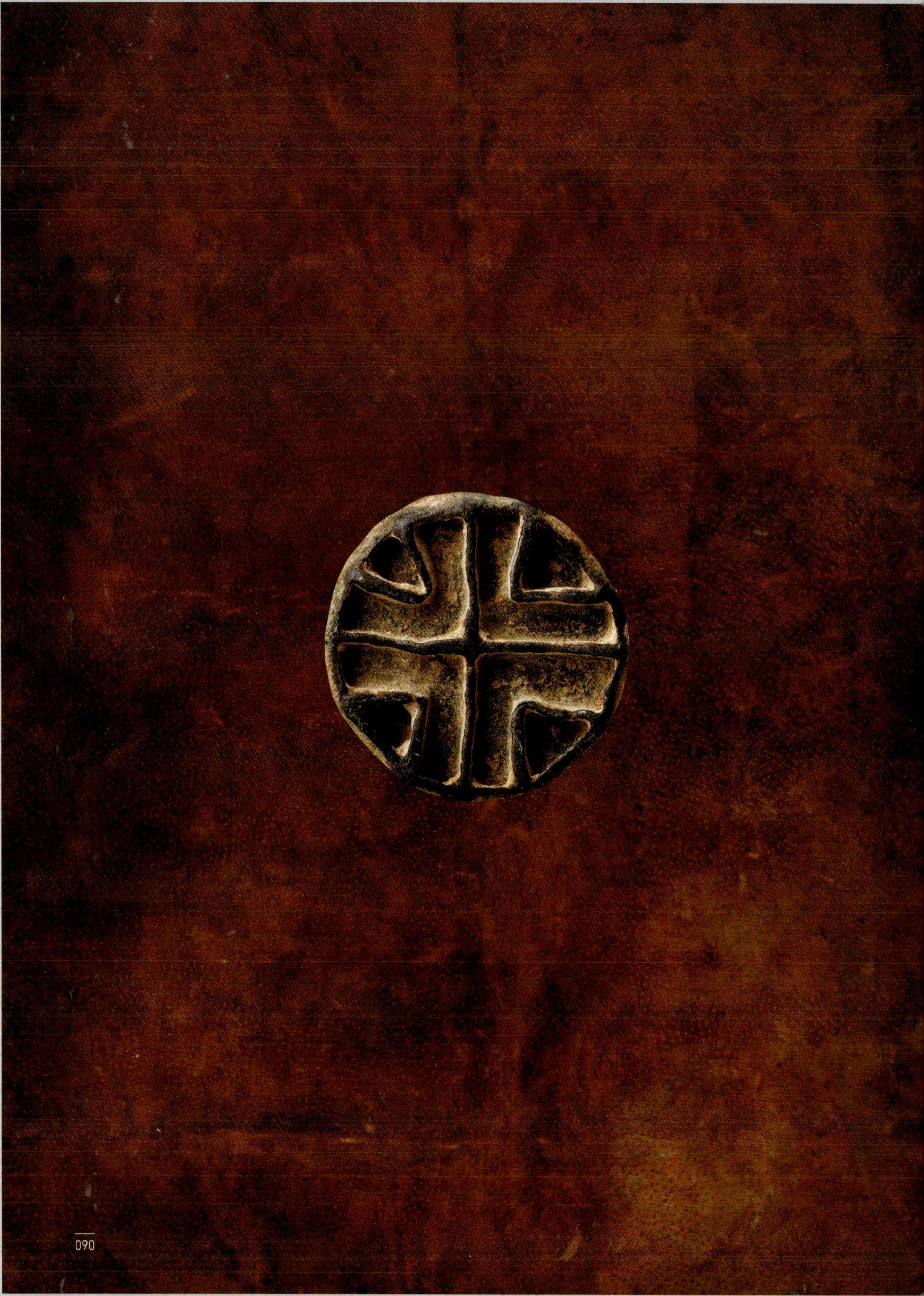

阿克瑟斯文明　Oxus Civilization　　121

| 题材 Subject Matter |
| 几何纹 Geometry Pattern |

121

阿克瑟斯文明　Oxus Civilization　　　122-124

题材
Subject Matter

几何纹
Geometry Pattern

122　　　　　　　　　123　　　　　　　　　124

阿克瑟斯文明 Oxus Civilization	125-126	题材 Subject Matter
		几何纹 Geometry Pattern

125

126

| 阿克瑟斯文明 Oxus Civilization | 127-128 | 题材 Subject Matter |
| | | 几何纹 Geometry Pattern |

127

128

阿克瑟斯文明 Oxus Civilization　129

题材
Subject Matter

几何纹
Geometry Pattern

129

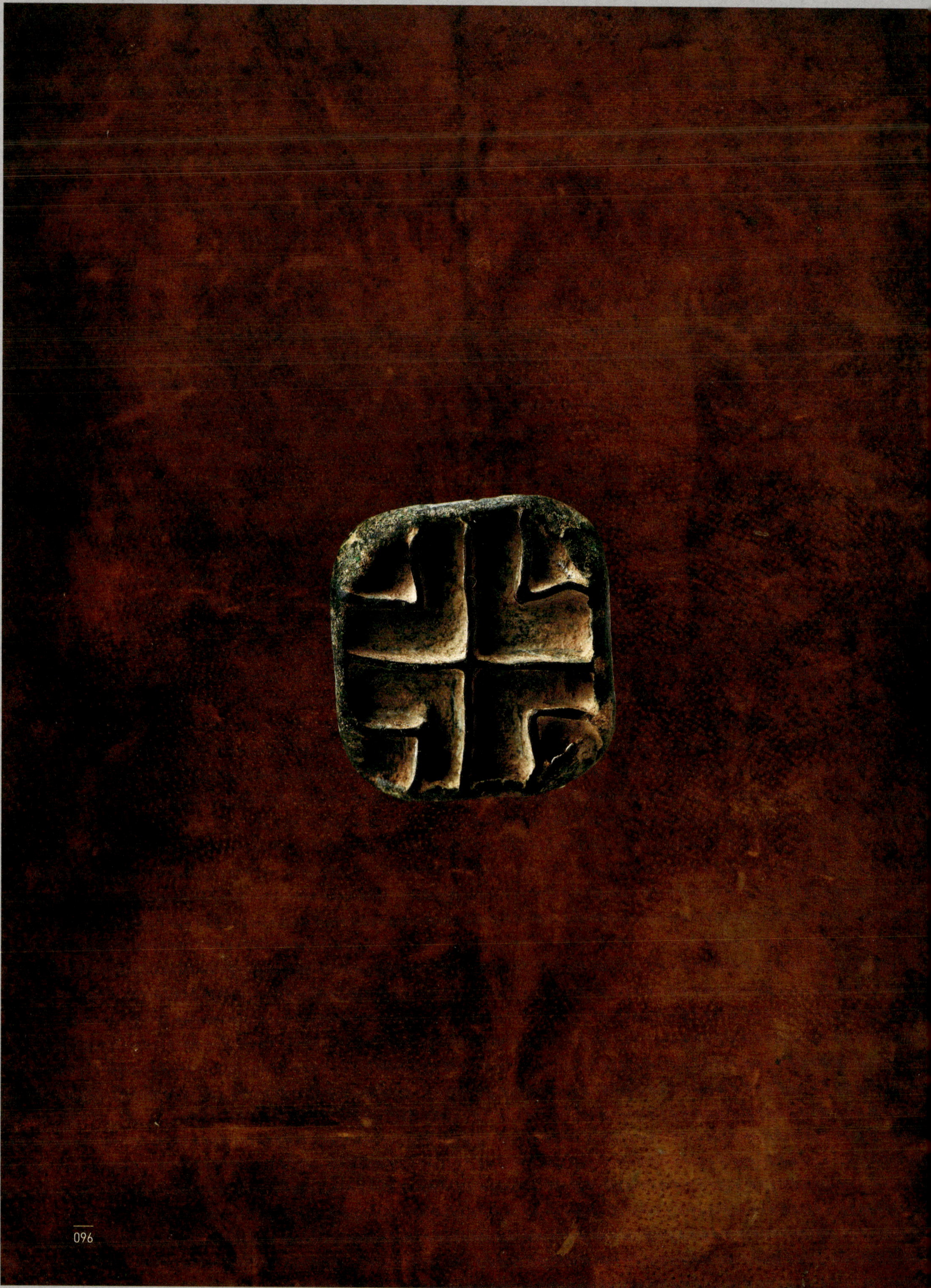

阿克瑟斯文明 Oxus Civilization　　130

题材
Subject Matter

几何纹
Geometry Pattern

130

| **阿克瑟斯文明** Oxus Civilization | 131-132 | 题材 Subject Matter |
| | | 几何纹 Geometry Pattern |

131

132

| 阿克瑟斯文明 Oxus Civilization | 133-134 | 题材 Subject Matter |
| | | 几何纹 Geometry Pattern |

133

134

| 阿克瑟斯文明 Oxus Civilization | 135 | 题材 Subject Matter |
| | | 几何纹 Geometry Pattern |

135

| 阿克瑟斯文明　Oxus Civilization | 136 | 题材　Subject Matter |
| | | 几何纹　Geometry Pattern |

136

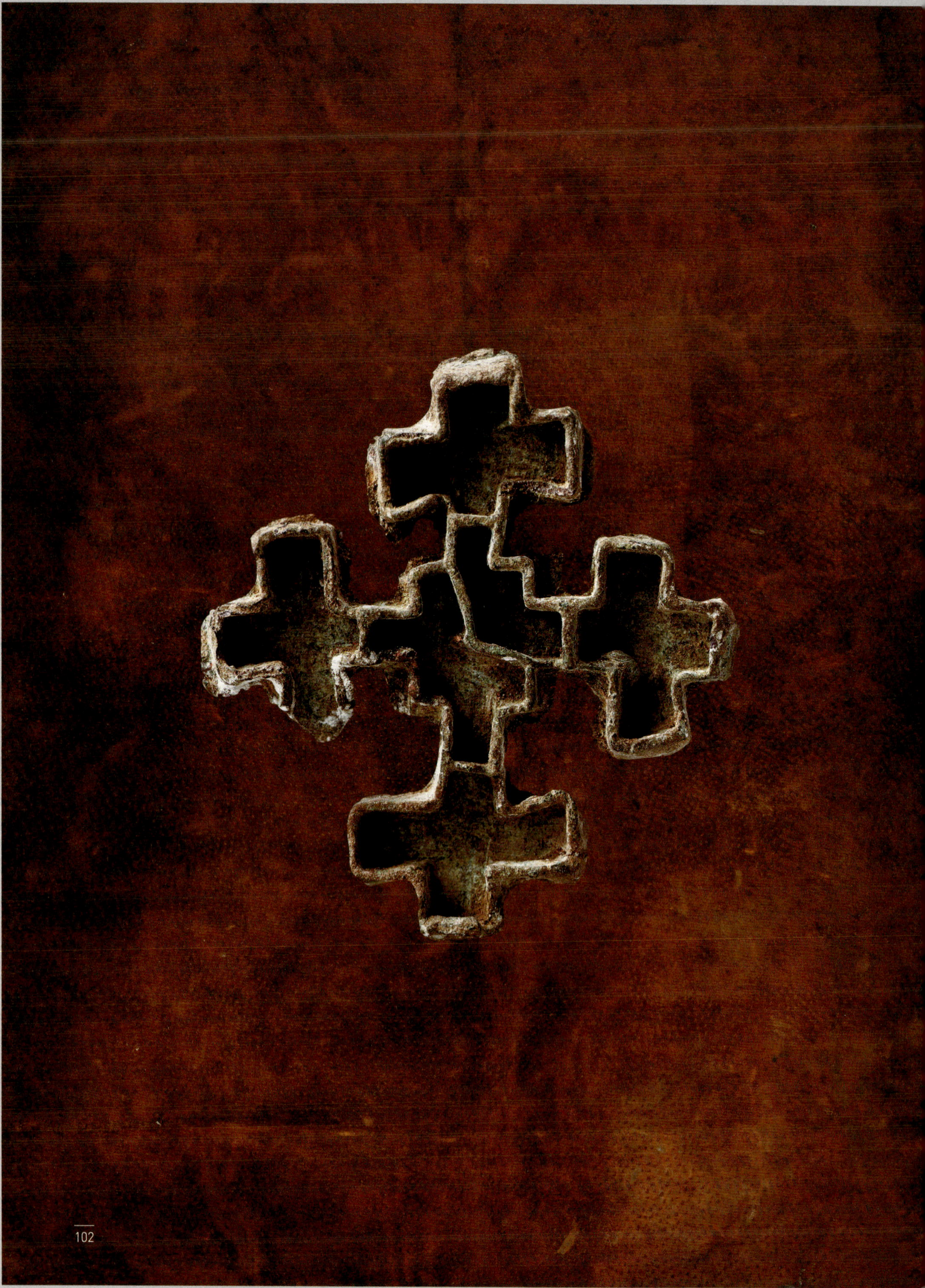

阿克瑟斯文明 Oxus Civilization 137

题材
Subject Matter

几何纹
Geometry Pattern

137

阿克瑟斯文明　Oxus Civilization

题材
Subject Matter

几何纹
Geometry Pattern

138

阿克瑟斯文明 Oxus Civilization

139

题材
Subject Matter

几何纹
Geometry Pattern

139

阿克瑟斯文明 Oxus Civilization

140-142

题材
Subject Matter

几何纹
Geometry Pattern

140

141

142

阿克瑟斯文明 Oxus Civilization

143

题材 Subject Matter
几何纹 Geometry Pattern

143

阿克瑟斯文明　Oxus Civilization

144

题材
Subject Matter

几何纹
Geometry Pattern

144

阿克瑟斯文明 Oxus Civilization

145

| 题材
Subject Matter

| 几何纹
Geometry Pattern

145

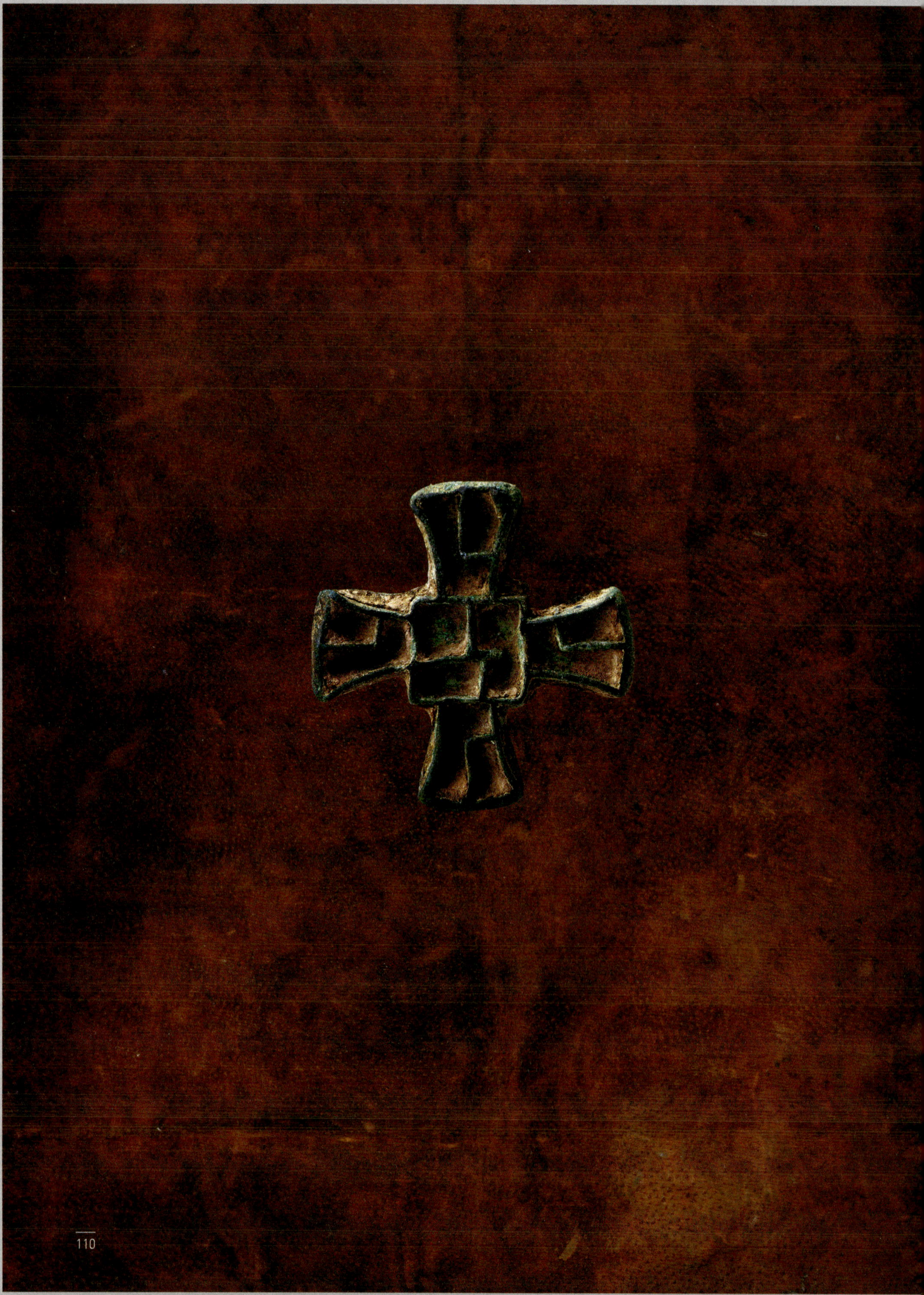

阿克瑟斯文明　Oxus Civilization

146

题材
Subject Matter

几何纹
Geometry Pattern

146

阿克瑟斯文明 Oxus Civilization   147-149   题材
Subject Matter

几何纹
Geometry Pattern

147

148

149

阿克瑟斯文明　Oxus Civilization	150-151	题材　Subject Matter
		几何纹　Geometry Pattern

150

151

| 阿克瑟斯文明 Oxus Civilization | 152-154 | 题材 Subject Matter |
| | | 几何纹 Geometry Pattern |

152

153

154

阿克瑟斯文明 Oxus Civilization　　155-157　　题材
　　　　　　　　　　　　　　　　　　　　　Subject Matter

　　　　　　　　　　　　　　　　　　　　　几何纹
　　　　　　　　　　　　　　　　　　　　　Geometry Pattern

155　　　　　　　　156　　　　　　　　157

| 阿克瑟斯文明 Oxus Civilization | 158-160 | 题材 Subject Matter |
| | | 几何纹 Geometry Pattern |

158

159

160

阿克瑟斯文明 Oxus Civilization　　161-165

题材
Subject Matter

几何纹
Geometry Pattern

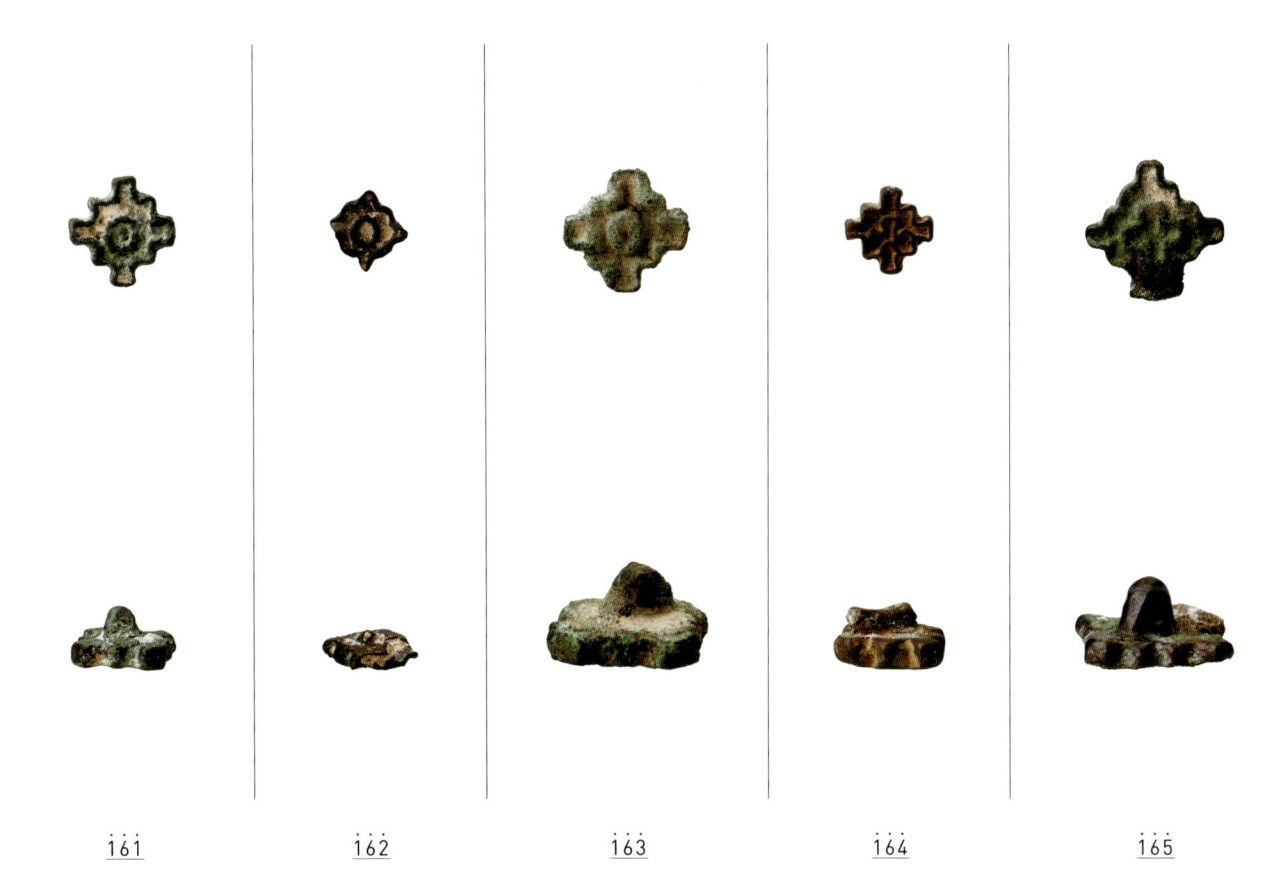

161　　162　　163　　164　　165

阿克瑟斯文明 Oxus Civilization	166-168	题材 Subject Matter
		几何纹 Geometry Pattern

166

167

168

阿克瑟斯文明　Oxus Civilization　　169

题材 Subject Matter
几何纹 Geometry Pattern

169

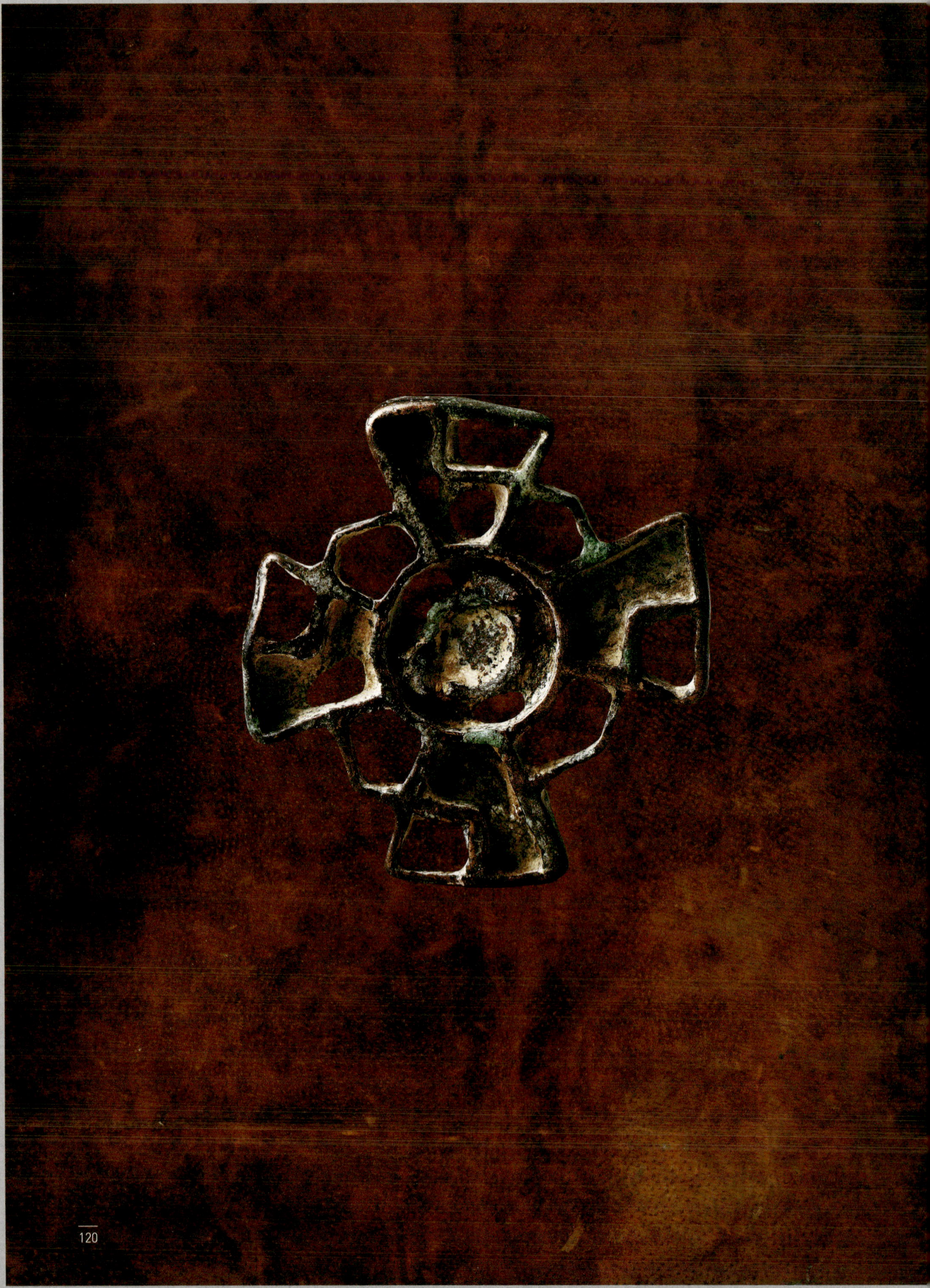

阿克瑟斯文明 Oxus Civilization   170

| 题材 Subject Matter |
| 几何纹 Geometry Pattern |

170

| 阿克瑟斯文明 Oxus Civilization | 171-172 | 题材 Subject Matter |
| | | 几何纹 Geometry Pattern |

171

172

阿克瑟斯文明 Oxus Civilization

173

| 题材
Subject Matter

| 几何纹
Geometry Pattern

173

| 阿克瑟斯文明 Oxus Civilization | 174-175 | 题材 Subject Matter |
| | | 几何纹 Geometry Pattern |

174

175

阿克瑟斯文明 Oxus Civilization　　176-177

| 题材
Subject Matter

| 几何纹
Geometry Pattern

176

177

阿克瑟斯文明 Oxus Civilization   178

题材
Subject Matter

几何纹
Geometry Pattern

178

| 阿克瑟斯文明 Oxus Civilization | 179 | 题材 Subject Matter |
| | | 几何纹 Geometry Pattern |

179

阿克瑟斯文明 Oxus Civilization   180

题材
Subject Matter

几何纹
Geometry Pattern

180

阿克瑟斯文明 Oxus Civilization	181-182	题材 Subject Matter
		几何纹 Geometry Pattern

181

182

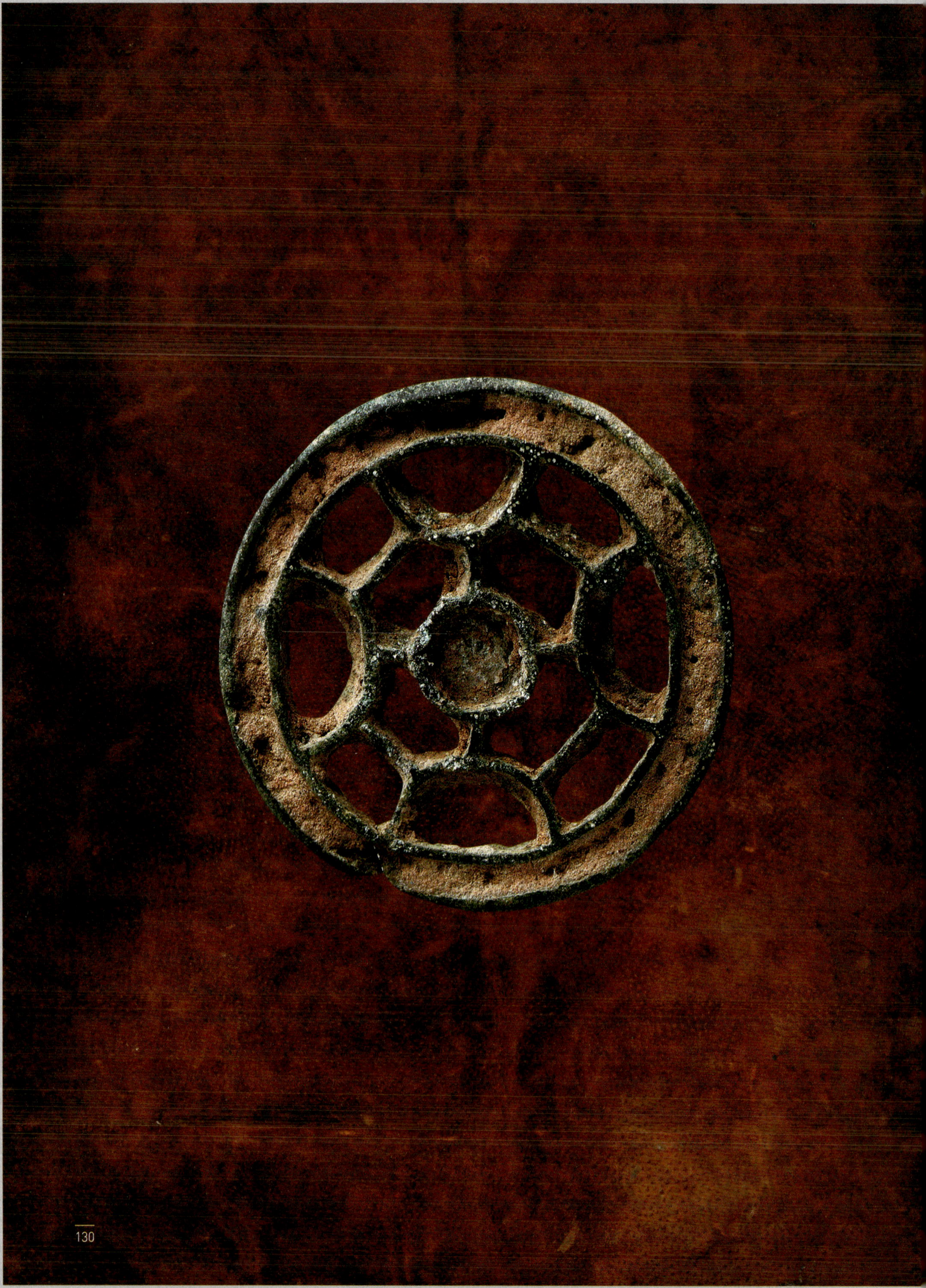

阿克瑟斯文明 Oxus Civilization

183

题材
Subject Matter

几何纹
Geometry Pattern

183

阿克瑟斯文明　Oxus Civilization	184-185	题材 Subject Matter
		几何纹 Geometry Pattern

184

185

阿克瑟斯文明 Oxus Civilization 186

| 题材 |
| Subject Matter |

| 几何纹 |
| Geometry Pattern |

186

| 阿克瑟斯文明 Oxus Civilization | 187-189 | 题材 Subject Matter |
| | | 几何纹 Geometry Pattern |

187

188

189

阿克瑟斯文明 Oxus Civilization

190

| 题材 Subject Matter |
| 几何纹 Geometry Pattern |

190

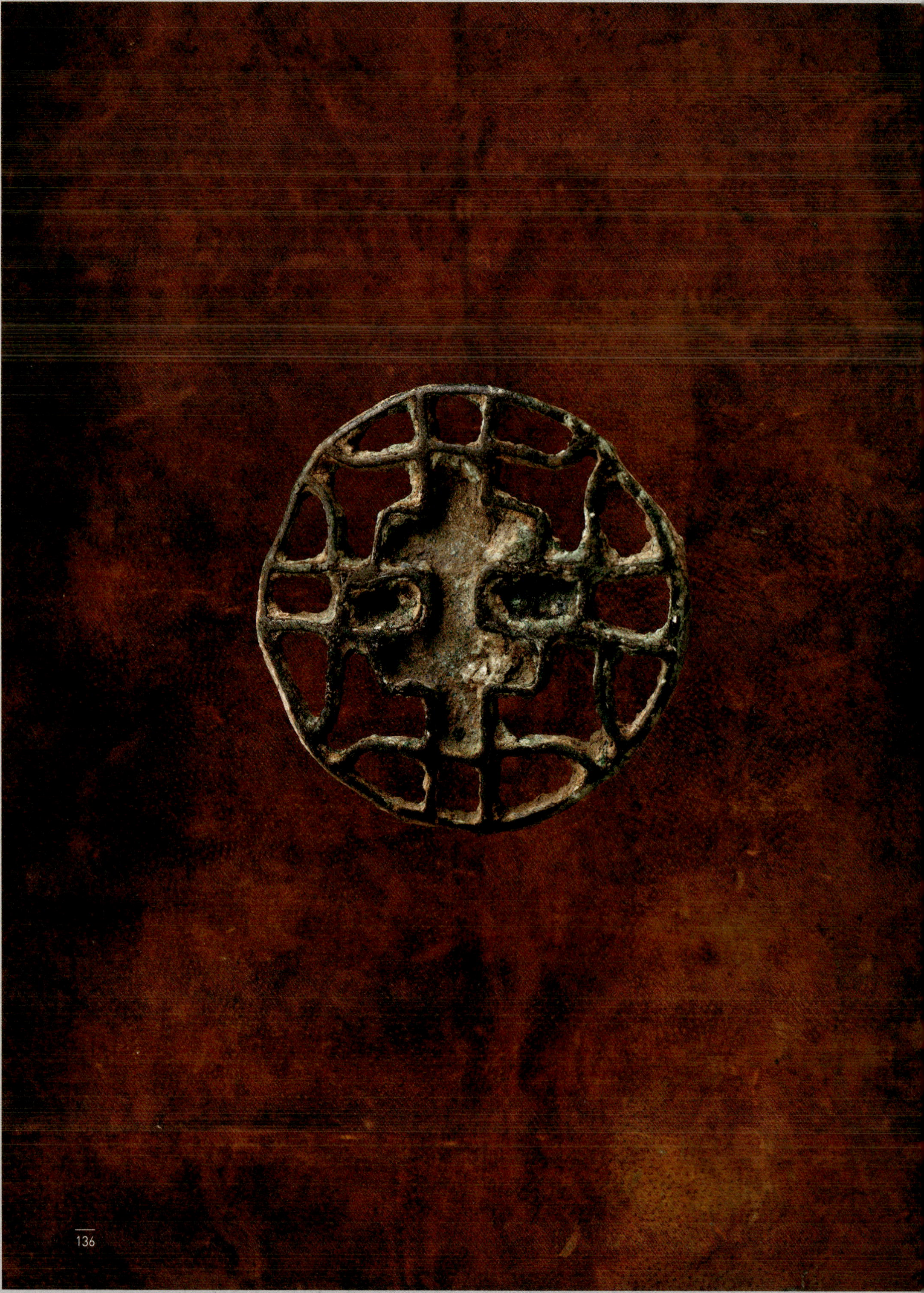

阿克瑟斯文明 Oxus Civilization

191

| 题材 Subject Matter
| 几何纹 Geometry Pattern

191

阿克瑟斯文明　Oxus Civilization	192-193	题材 Subject Matter
		几何纹 Geometry Pattern

192

193

阿克瑟斯文明 Oxus Civilization 194-195

题材
Subject Matter

几何纹
Geometry Pattern

194

195

阿克瑟斯文明　Oxus Civilization　196

题材
Subject Matter

几何纹
Geometry Pattern

196

| 阿克瑟斯文明　Oxus Civilization | 197 | 题材　Subject Matter |
| | | 几何纹　Geometry Pattern |

197

阿克瑟斯文明 Oxus Civilization	198-199	题材 Subject Matter
		几何纹 Geometry Pattern

198

199

阿克瑟斯文明　Oxus Civilization　200

题材
Subject Matter

几何纹
Geometry Pattern

200

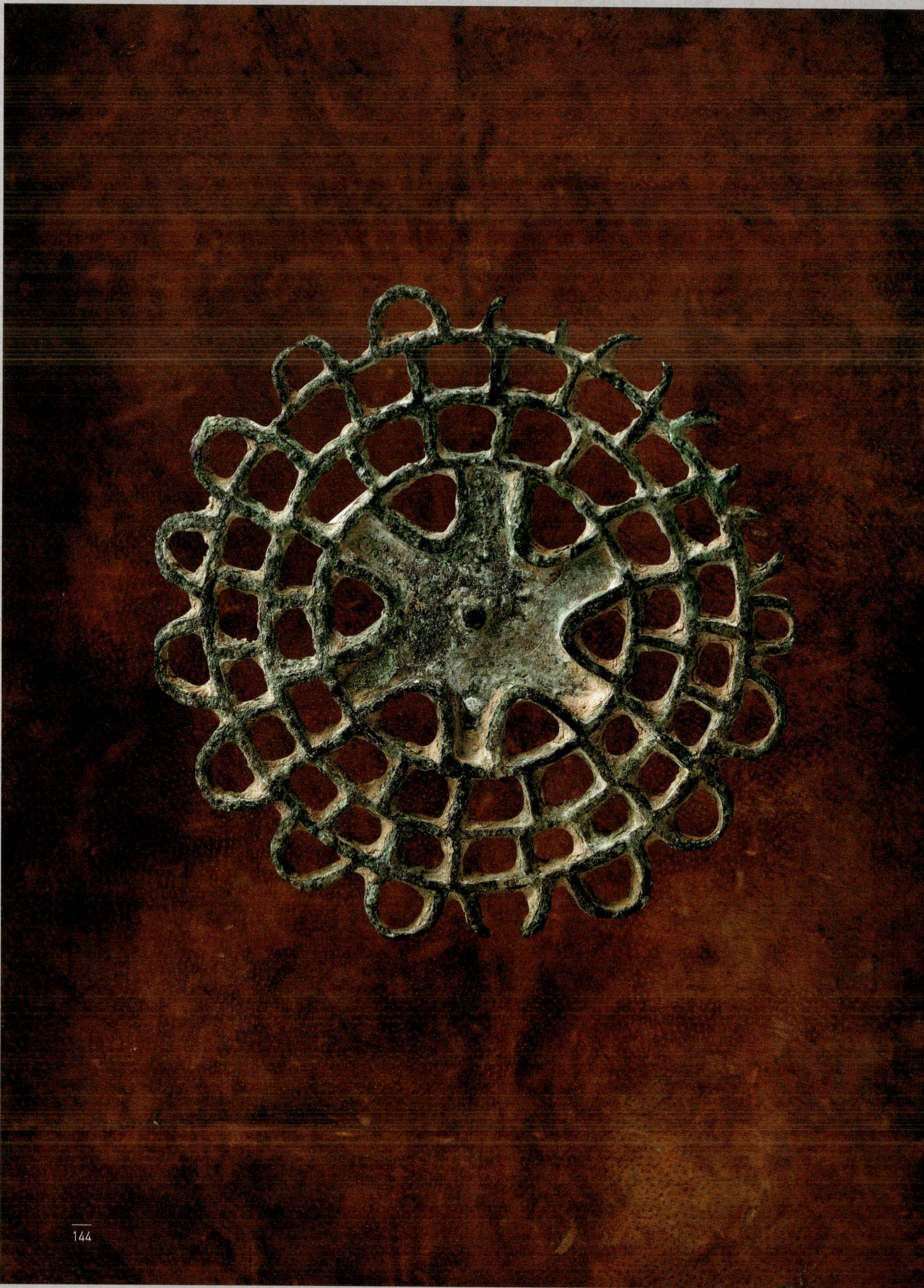

阿克瑟斯文明 Oxus Civilization

201

| 题材 Subject Matter |
| 几何纹 Geometry Pattern |

201

| 阿克瑟斯文明 Oxus Civilization | 202-203 | 题材 Subject Matter |
| | | 几何纹 Geometry Pattern |

202

203

阿克瑟斯文明 Oxus Civilization 204

题材 Subject Matter
几何纹 Geometry Pattern

204

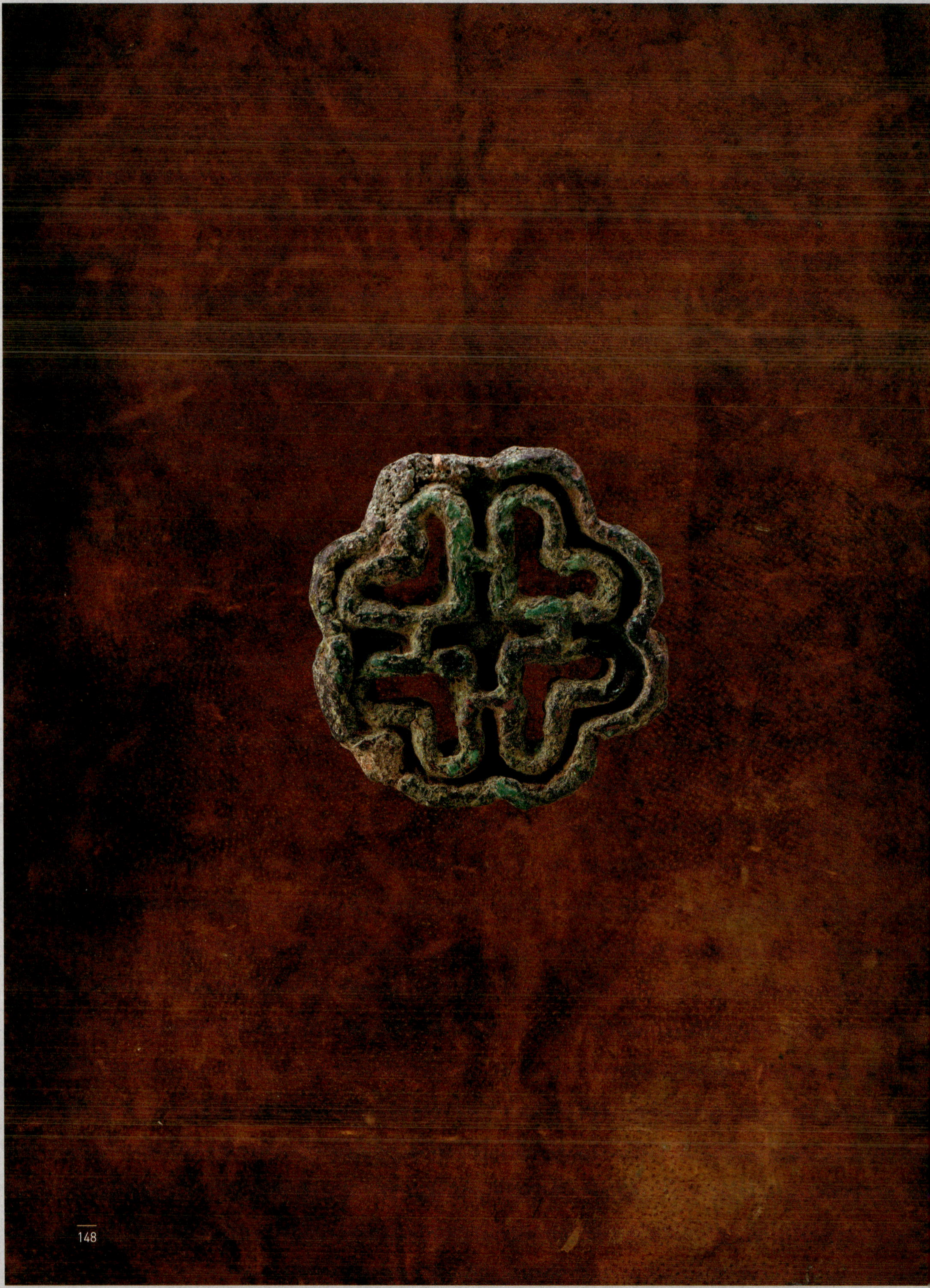

阿克瑟斯文明 Oxus Civilization

205

题材
Subject Matter

几何纹
Geometry Pattern

205

阿克瑟斯文明　Oxus Civilization　　206-207

题材
Subject Matter

几何纹
Geometry Pattern

206

207

阿克瑟斯文明 Oxus Civilization

208

| 题材 Subject Matter |
| 几何纹 Geometry Pattern |

208

阿克瑟斯文明 Oxus Civilization

209

| 题材 Subject Matter |
| 几何纹 Geometry Pattern |

209

阿克瑟斯文明　Oxus Civilization

210

| 题材 Subject Matter |
| 几何纹 Geometry Pattern |

210

阿克瑟斯文明 Oxus Civilization

211

题材
Subject Matter

几何纹
Geometry Pattern

211

阿克瑟斯文明 Oxus Civilization

212

题材 Subject Matter
几何纹 Geometry Pattern

212

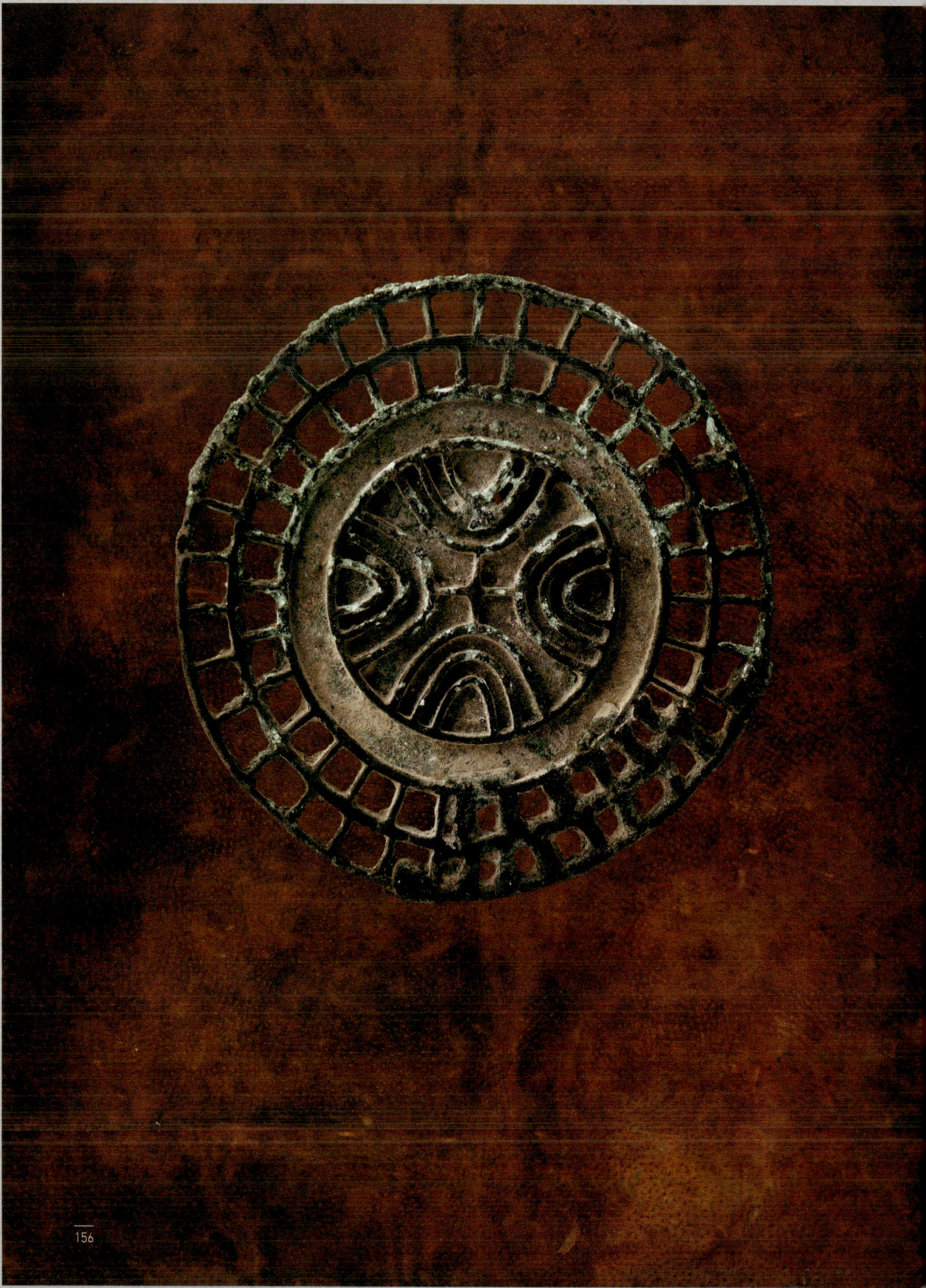

阿克瑟斯文明　Oxus Civilization

213

| 题材
| Subject Matter

| 几何纹
| Geometry Pattern

213

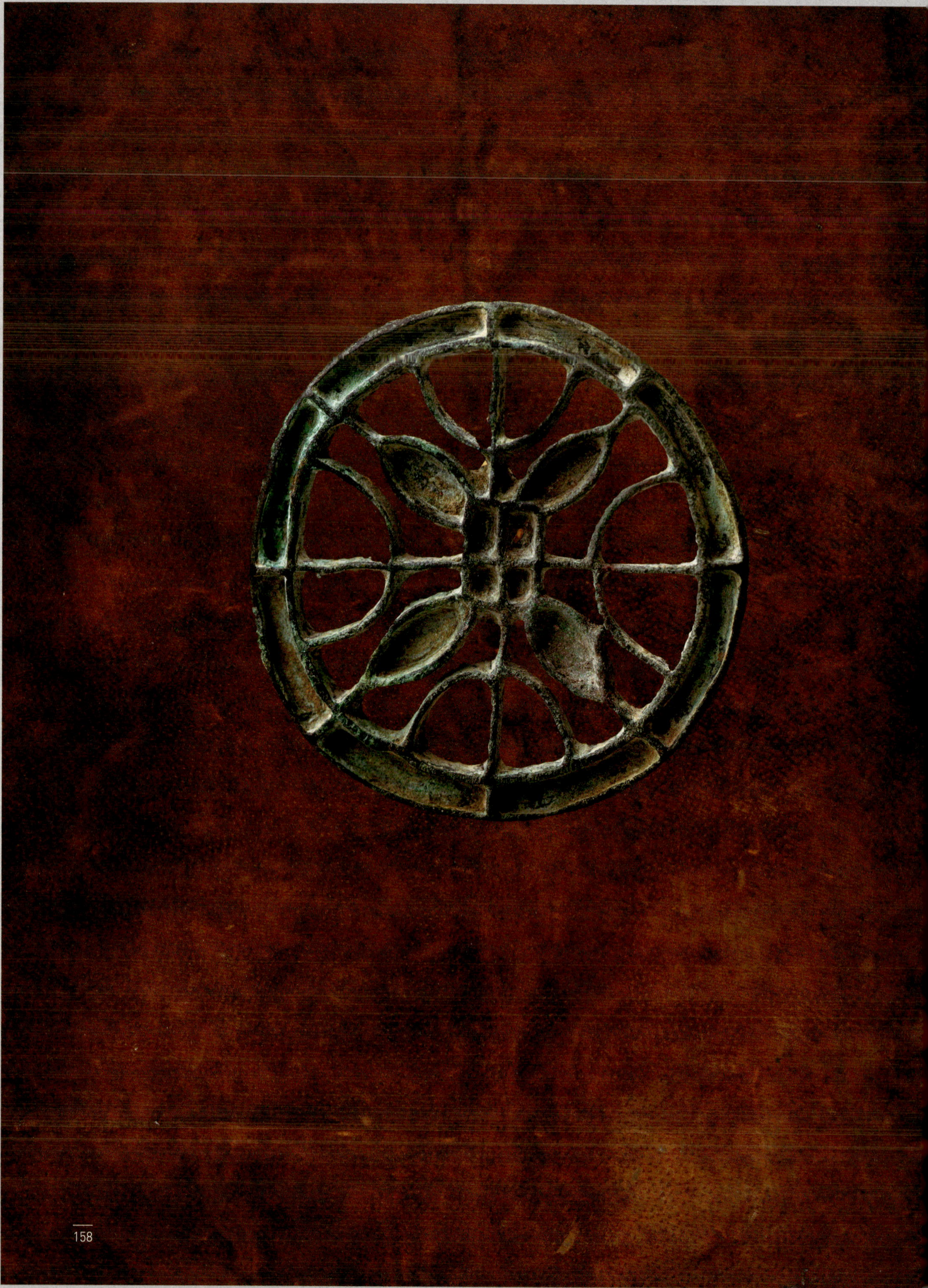

阿克瑟斯文明 Oxus Civilization

214

题材 Subject Matter
植物 Plant

214

阿克瑟斯文明　Oxus Civilization

215

题材
Subject Matter

植物
Plant

215

阿克瑟斯文明 Oxus Civilization 216

题材
Subject Matter

植物
Plant

216

| 阿克瑟斯文明　Oxus Civilization | 217-218 | 题材　Subject Matter |
| | | 植物　Plant |

217

218

阿克瑟斯文明 Oxus Civilization

219

题材
Subject Matter

植物
Plant

219

阿克瑟斯文明　Oxus Civilization　　220　　題材
Subject Matter

植物
Plant

220

阿克瑟斯文明　Oxus Civilization

221

题材 Subject Matter
植物 Plant

221

阿克瑟斯文明 Oxus Civilization

222

题材 Subject Matter
植物 Plant

222

阿克瑟斯文明　Oxus Civilization

223

题材
Subject Matter

植物
Plant

223

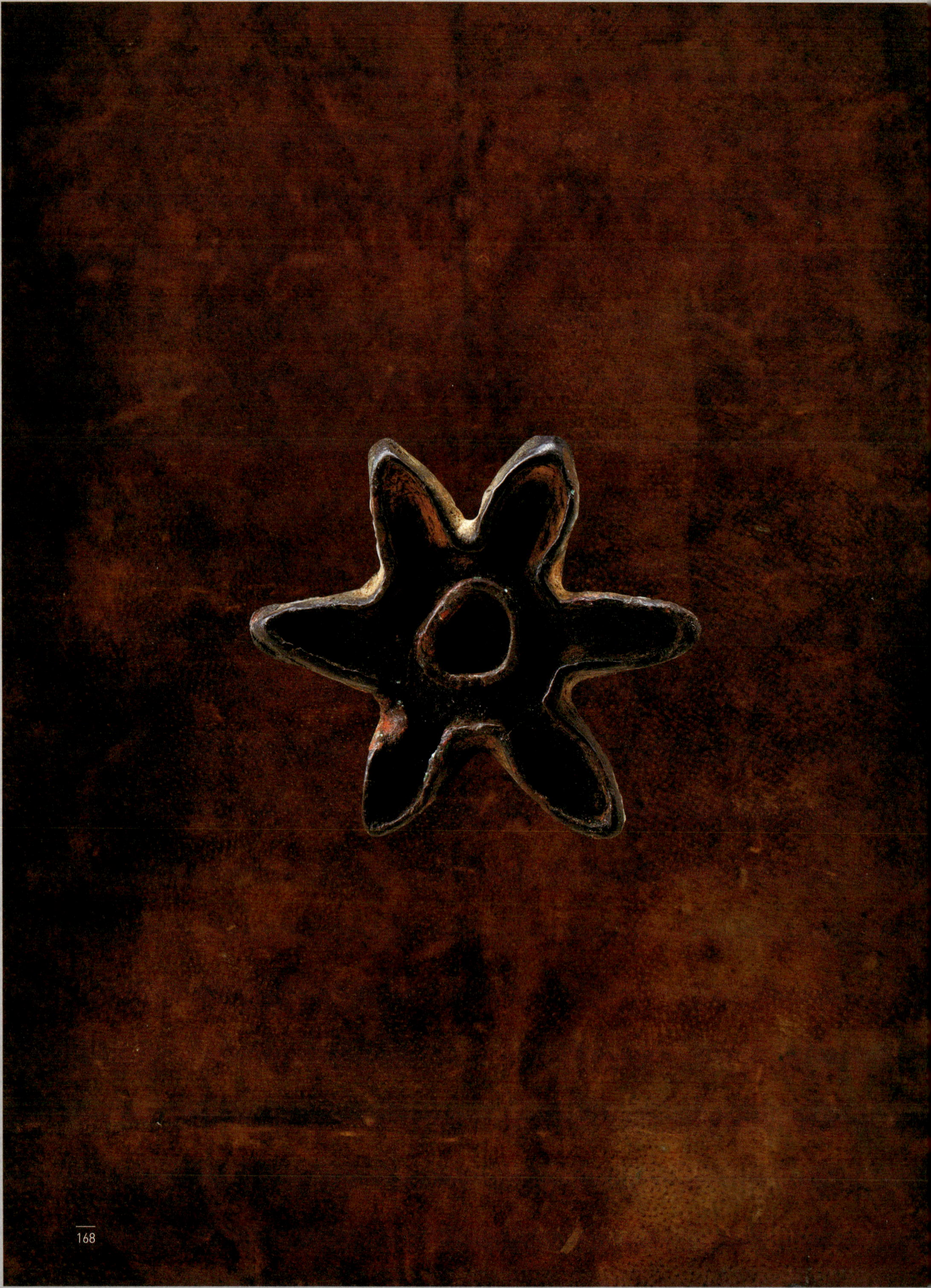

阿克瑟斯文明　Oxus Civilization

224

题材 Subject Matter
植物 Plant

224

阿克瑟斯文明 Oxus Civilization   225-227 | 题材
Subject Matter

| 植物
Plant

225 226 227

阿克瑟斯文明 Oxus Civilization　　228-229

| 题材
| Subject Matter
|
| 植物
| Plant

228

229

阿克瑟斯文明 Oxus Civilization 230-231

题材
Subject Matter

植物
Plant

230

231

阿克瑟斯文明 Oxus Civilization 232-240

题材
Subject Matter

植物
Plant

232　233　234　235　236

237　238　239　240

阿克瑟斯文明　Oxus Civilization	241-245	题材　Subject Matter
		植物　Plant

241

242

243

244

245

阿克瑟斯文明 Oxus Civilization 246-249

题材 Subject Matter
植物 Plant

246

247

248

249

阿克瑟斯文明 Oxus Civilization　　250

题材
Subject Matter

植物
Plant

250

阿克瑟斯文明 Oxus Civilization 251-252

| 题材
| Subject Matter
|
| 植物
| Plant

251

252

阿克瑟斯文明 Oxus Civilization 253 | 题材 Subject Matter
| 铭文 Inscription

253

阿克瑟斯文明 Oxus Civilization 254-256

| 题材 Subject Matter
| 铭文 Inscription

254

255

256

阿克瑟斯文明　Oxus Civilization　257-265

| 题材
Subject Matter

| 铭文
Inscription

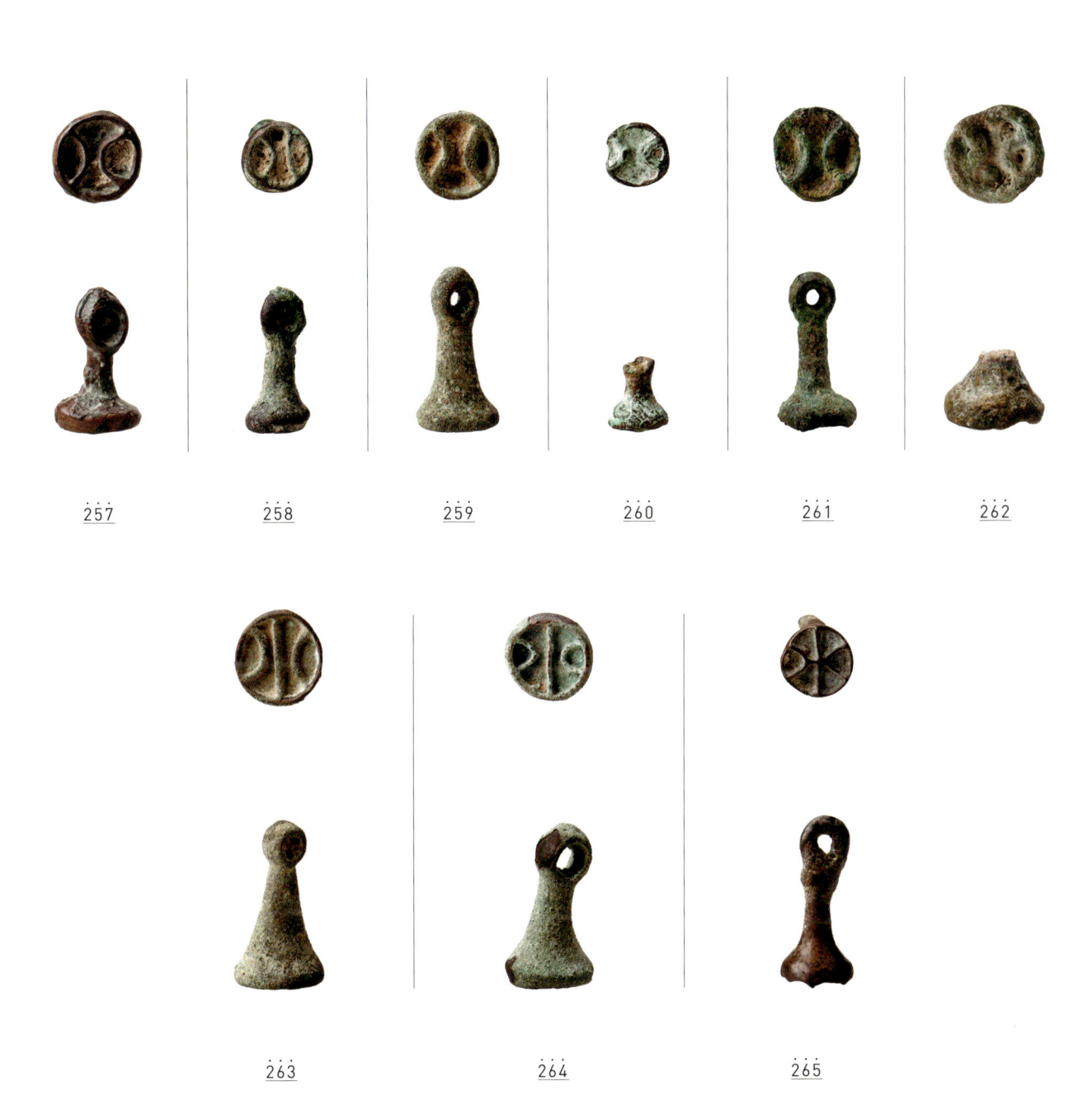

257　258　259　260　261　262

263　264　265

| 阿克瑟斯文明 Oxus Civilization | 266-268 | 题材 Subject Matter |
| | | 铭文 Inscription |

266

267

268

阿克瑟斯文明 Oxus Civilization 269-274

| 题材 Subject Matter |
| 铭文 Inscription |

269

270

271

272

273

274

183

| 阿克瑟斯文明 Oxus Civilization | 275-277 | 题材 Subject Matter |
| | | 铭文 Inscription |

275

276

277

阿克瑟斯文明 Oxus Civilization

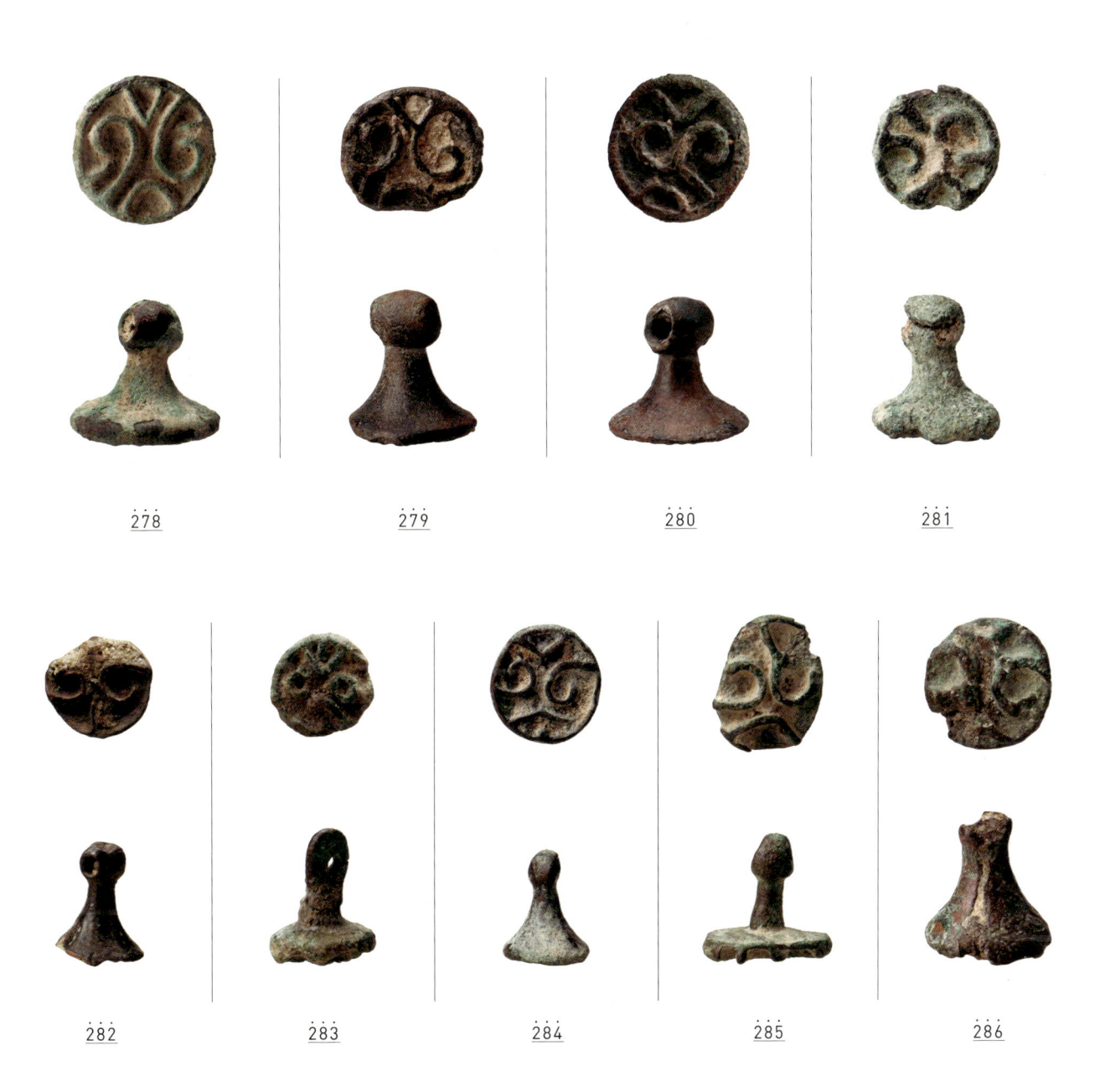

278-286

| 题材 Subject Matter |
| 铭文 Inscription |

278

279

280

281

282

283

284

285

286

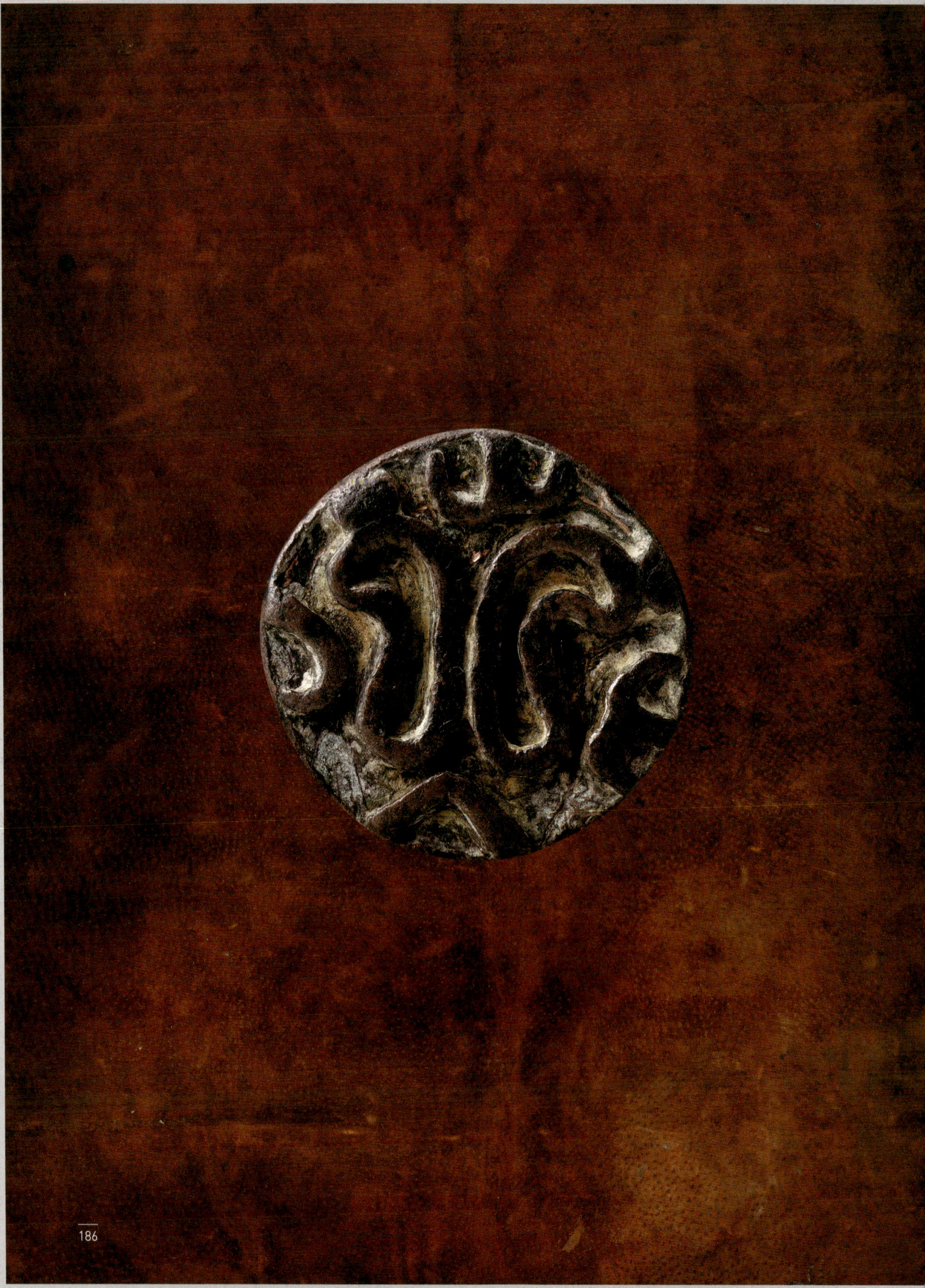

阿克瑟斯文明　Oxus Civilization

287

题材 Subject Matter
铭文 Inscription

287

阿克瑟斯文明 Oxus Civilization   288-289 | 题材
Subject Matter

| 铭文
Inscription

288

289

阿克瑟斯文明　Oxus Civilization   290-291 | 题材
Subject Matter

| 铭文
Inscription

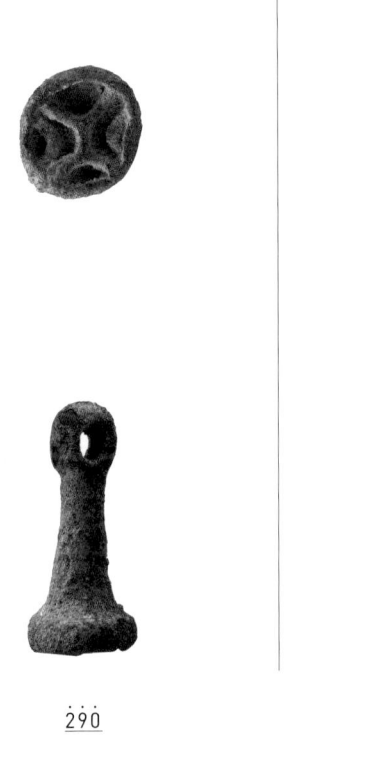

290

291

阿克瑟斯文明　Oxus Civilization　292-293

题材
Subject Matter

铭文
Inscription

292

293

| 阿克瑟斯文明 Oxus Civilization | 294-295 | 题材 Subject Matter |
| | | 铭文 Inscription |

294

295

阿克瑟斯文明 Oxus Civilization

296-299

题材
Subject Matter

铭文
Inscription

296

297

298

299

阿克瑟斯文明 Oxus Civilization　　300-302

| 题材 Subject Matter |
| 铭文 Inscription |

300

301

302

阿克瑟斯文明 Oxus Civilization 303-304

题材
Subject Matter

铭文
Inscription

303

304

阿克瑟斯文明 Oxus Civilization

305-306

| 题材 Subject Matter |
| 铭文 Inscription |

305

306

阿克瑟斯文明　Oxus Civilization

307

| 题材 Subject Matter |
| 铭文 Inscription |

307

阿克瑟斯文明　Oxus Civilization　308

题材 Subject Matter	
铭文 Inscription	

308

阿克瑟斯文明 Oxus Civilization	309-311	题材 Subject Matter
		铭文 Inscription

309

310

311

阿克瑟斯文明 Oxus Civilization

312-316

| 题材
Subject Matter

| 铭文
Inscription

312   313   314   315   316

阿克瑟斯文明 Oxus Civilization　　317-320

| 题材
| Subject Matter

| 铭文
| Inscription

317　　318　　319　　320

阿克瑟斯文明 Oxus Civilization 321-322

| 题材 Subject Matter |
| 铭文 Inscription |

321

322

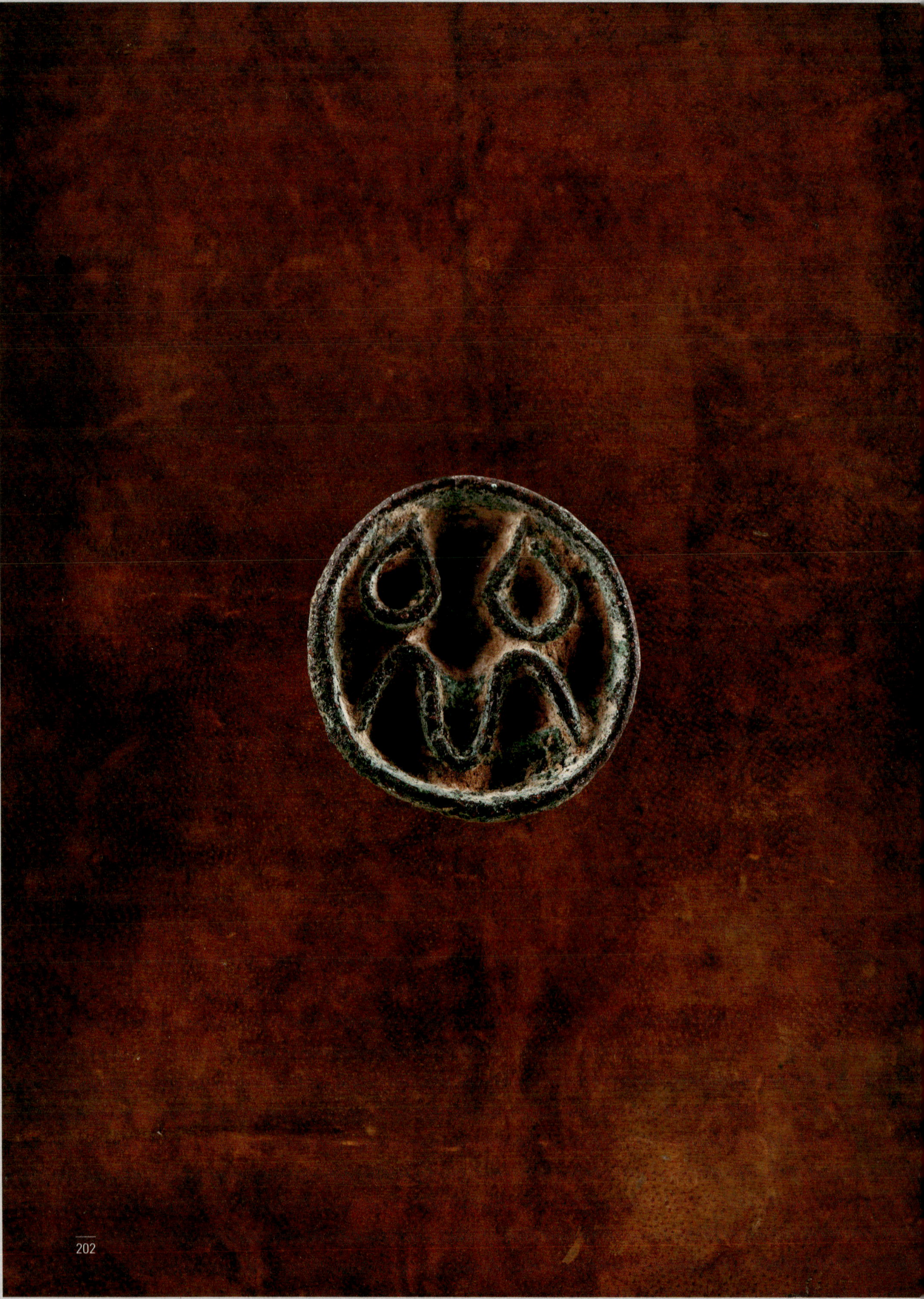

阿克瑟斯文明　Oxus Civilization

323

题材 Subject Matter
铭文 Inscription

323

阿克瑟斯文明 Oxus Civilization

324

题材
Subject Matter

铭文
Inscription

324

阿克瑟斯文明 Oxus Civilization

325

| 题材 Subject Matter |
| 铭文 Inscription |

325

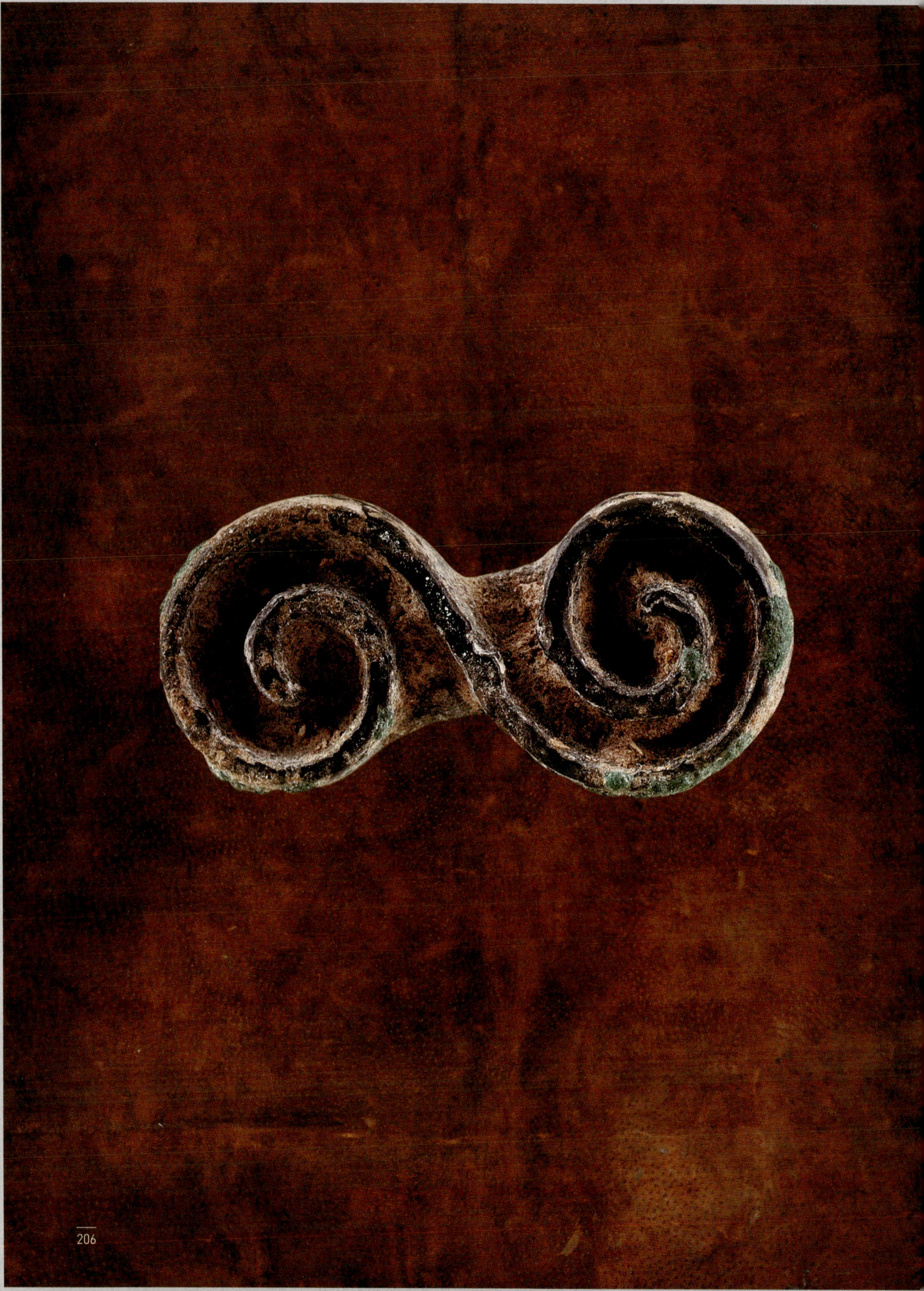

阿克瑟斯文明　Oxus Civilization

326

题材 Subject Matter
几何纹 Geometry Pattern

326

阿克瑟斯文明 Oxus Civilization 327-328

题材 | Subject Matter

几何纹 | Geometry Pattern

327

328

| 阿克瑟斯文明　Oxus Civilization | 329-330 | 题材
Subject Matter

几何纹
Geometry Pattern |

329

330

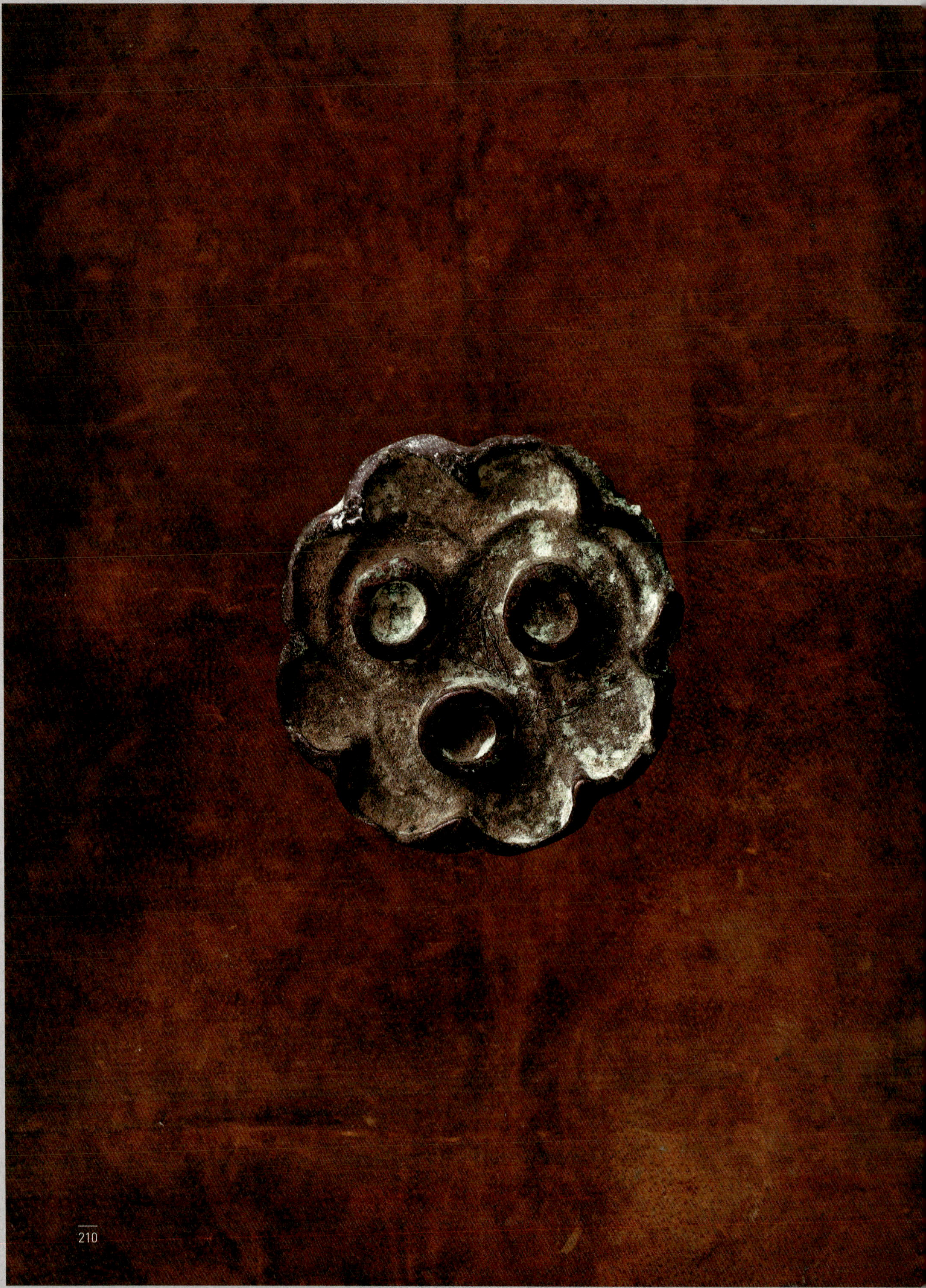

阿克瑟斯文明 Oxus Civilization

331

| 题材 Subject Matter |
| 几何纹 Geometry Pattern |

331

阿克瑟斯文明　Oxus Civilization	332-333	题材　Subject Matter
		几何纹　Geometry Pattern

332

333

阿克瑟斯文明 Oxus Civilization	334-335	题材 Subject Matter
		几何纹 Geometry Pattern

334

335

| 阿克瑟斯文明 Oxus Civilization | 336-338 | 题材 Subject Matter |
| | | 几何纹 Geometry Pattern |

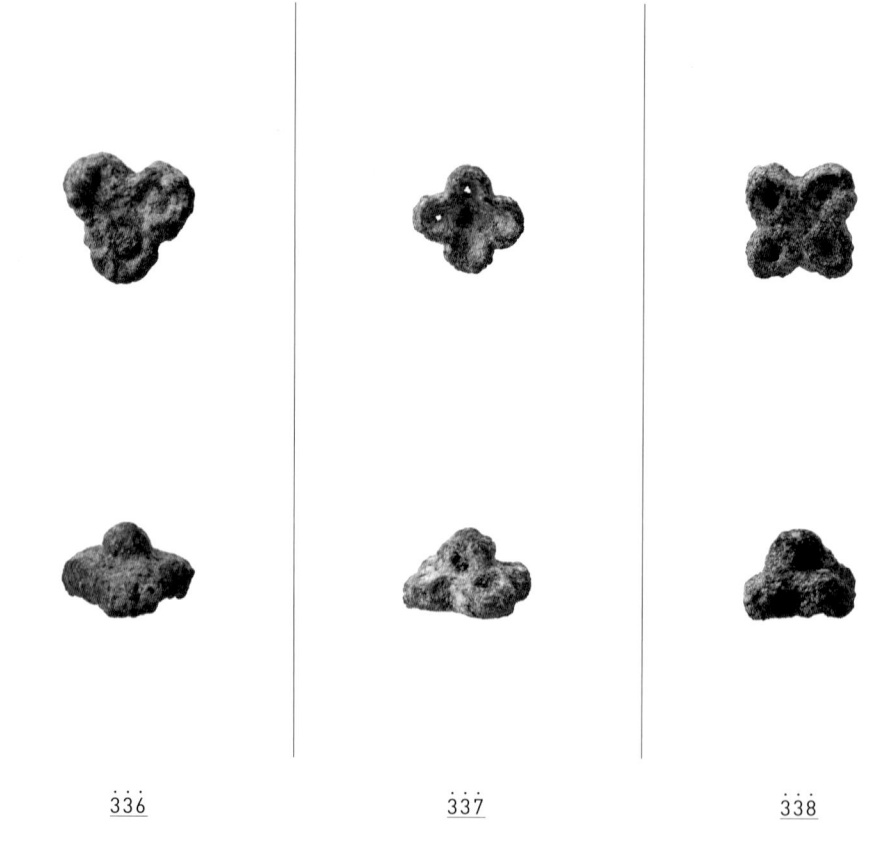

336

337

338

阿克瑟斯文明 Oxus Civilization

339

| 题材 Subject Matter |
| 几何纹 Geometry Pattern |

339

阿克瑟斯文明 Oxus Civilization　　340-341

题材
Subject Matter

几何纹
Geometry Pattern

340

341

216

阿克瑟斯文明 Oxus Civilization 342-344

题材
Subject Matter

几何纹
Geometry Pattern

342

343

344

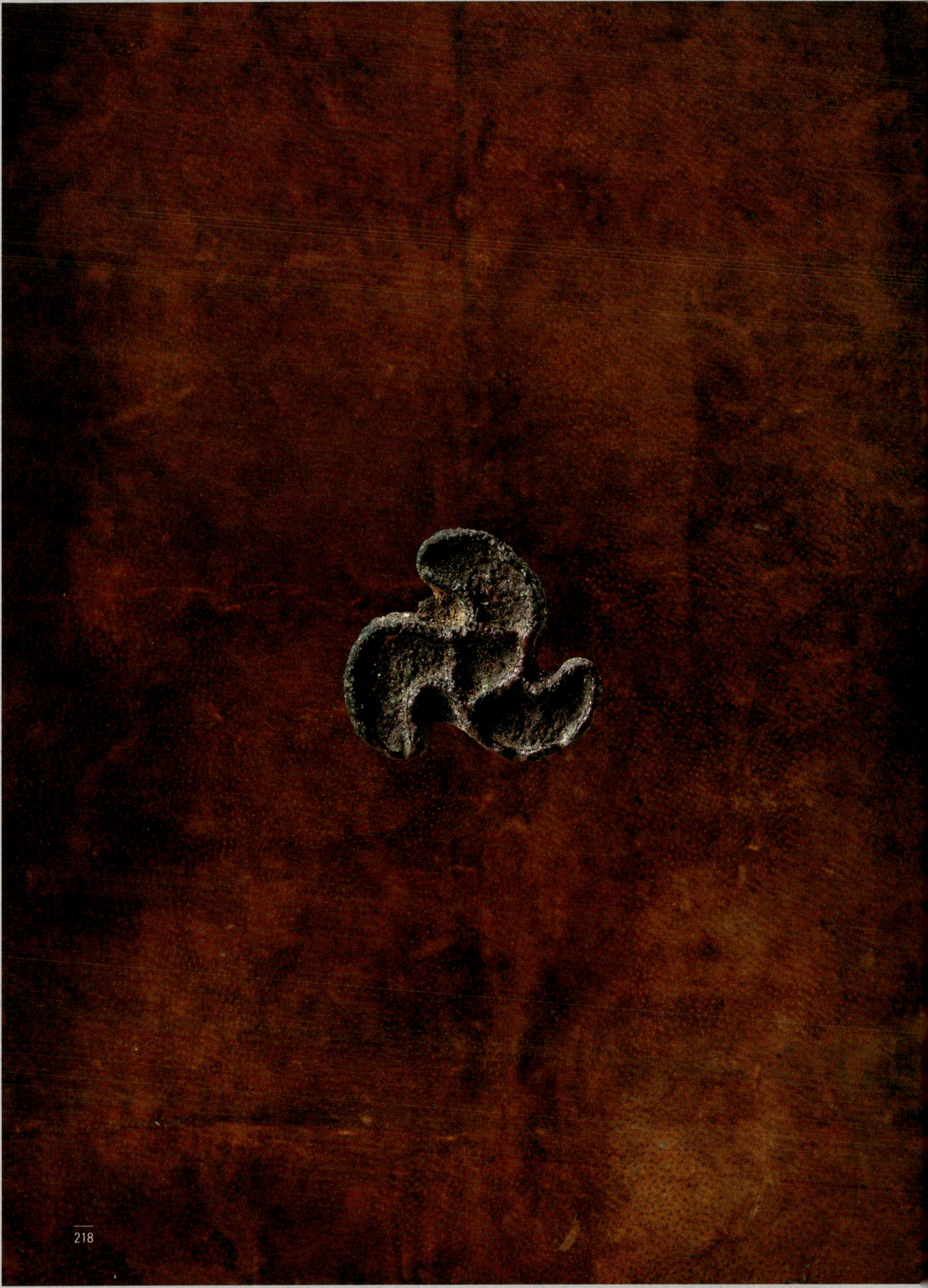

阿克瑟斯文明　Oxus Civilization

345

题材 Subject Matter
几何纹 Geometry Pattern

345

| 阿克瑟斯文明 Oxus Civilization | 346-347 | 题材 Subject Matter |
| | | 几何纹 Geometry Pattern |

346

347

阿克瑟斯文明 Oxus Civilization

348-350

| 题材
Subject Matter

| 几何纹
Geometry Pattern

348

349

350

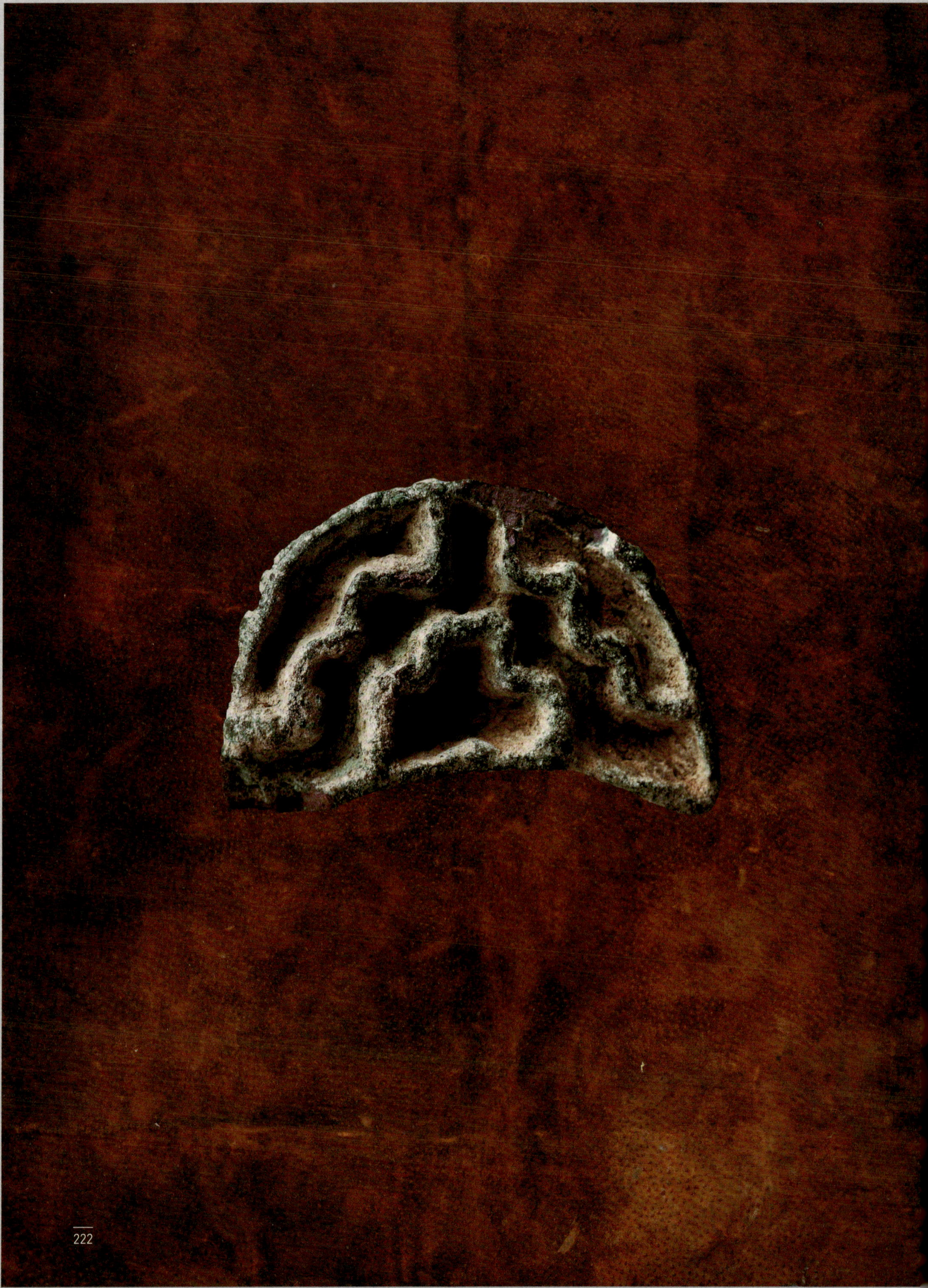

阿克瑟斯文明 Oxus Civilization

351

| 题材 Subject Matter |
| 铭文 Inscription |

351

阿克瑟斯文明 Oxus Civilization 352-356

题材
Subject Matter

铭文
Inscription

352   353   354   355   356

阿克瑟斯文明 Oxus Civilization	357-358	题材 Subject Matter
		铭文 Inscription

357

358

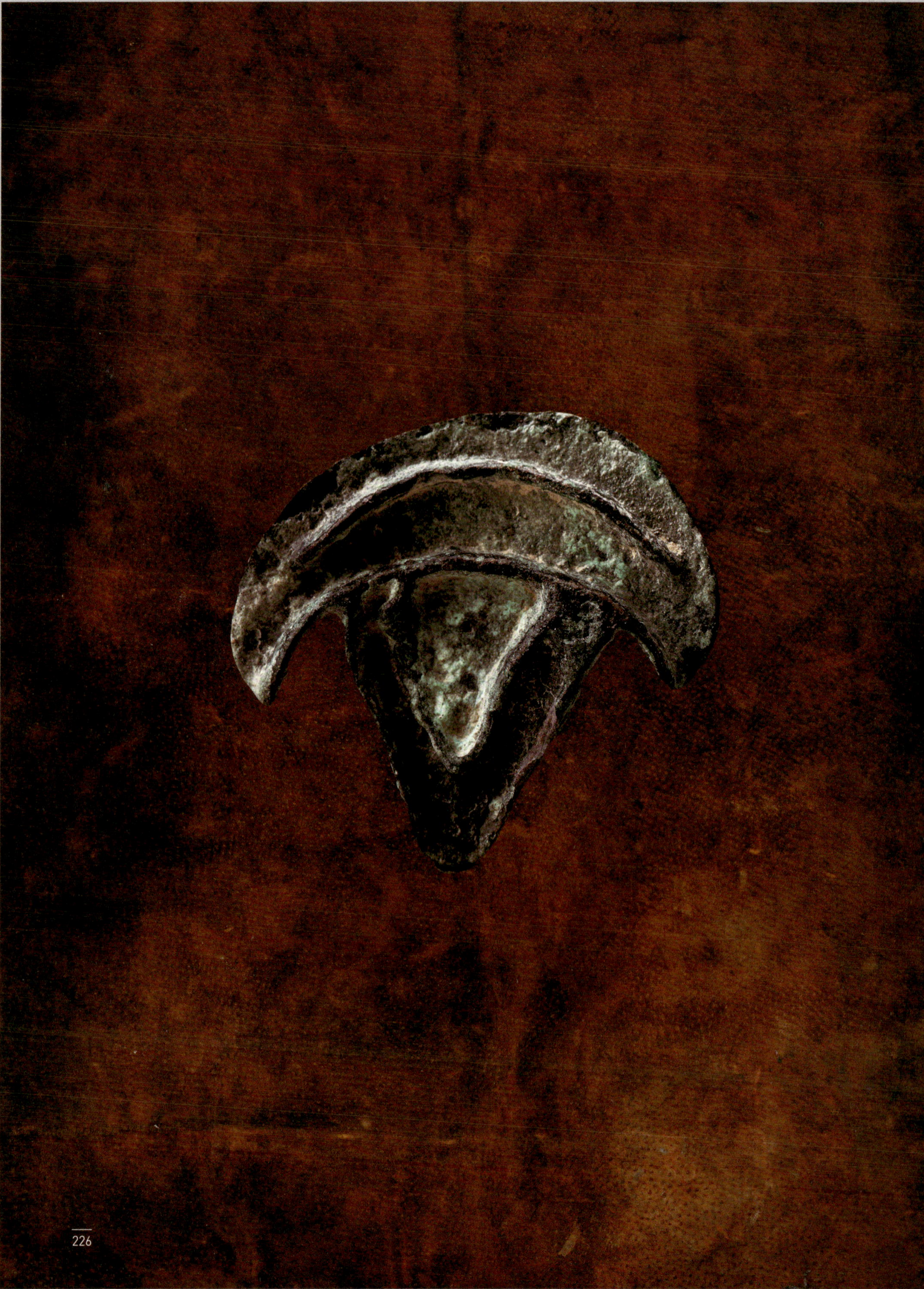

阿克瑟斯文明 Oxus Civilization

359

| 题材 Subject Matter |
| 铭文 Inscription |

359

| 阿克瑟斯文明 Oxus Civilization | 360 | 题材 Subject Matter |
| | | 铭文 Inscription |

360

阿克瑟斯文明 Oxus Civilization 　　361-362　　| 题材 Subject Matter
　　　　　　　　　　　　　　　　　　　　　　　　| 铭文 Inscription

361

362

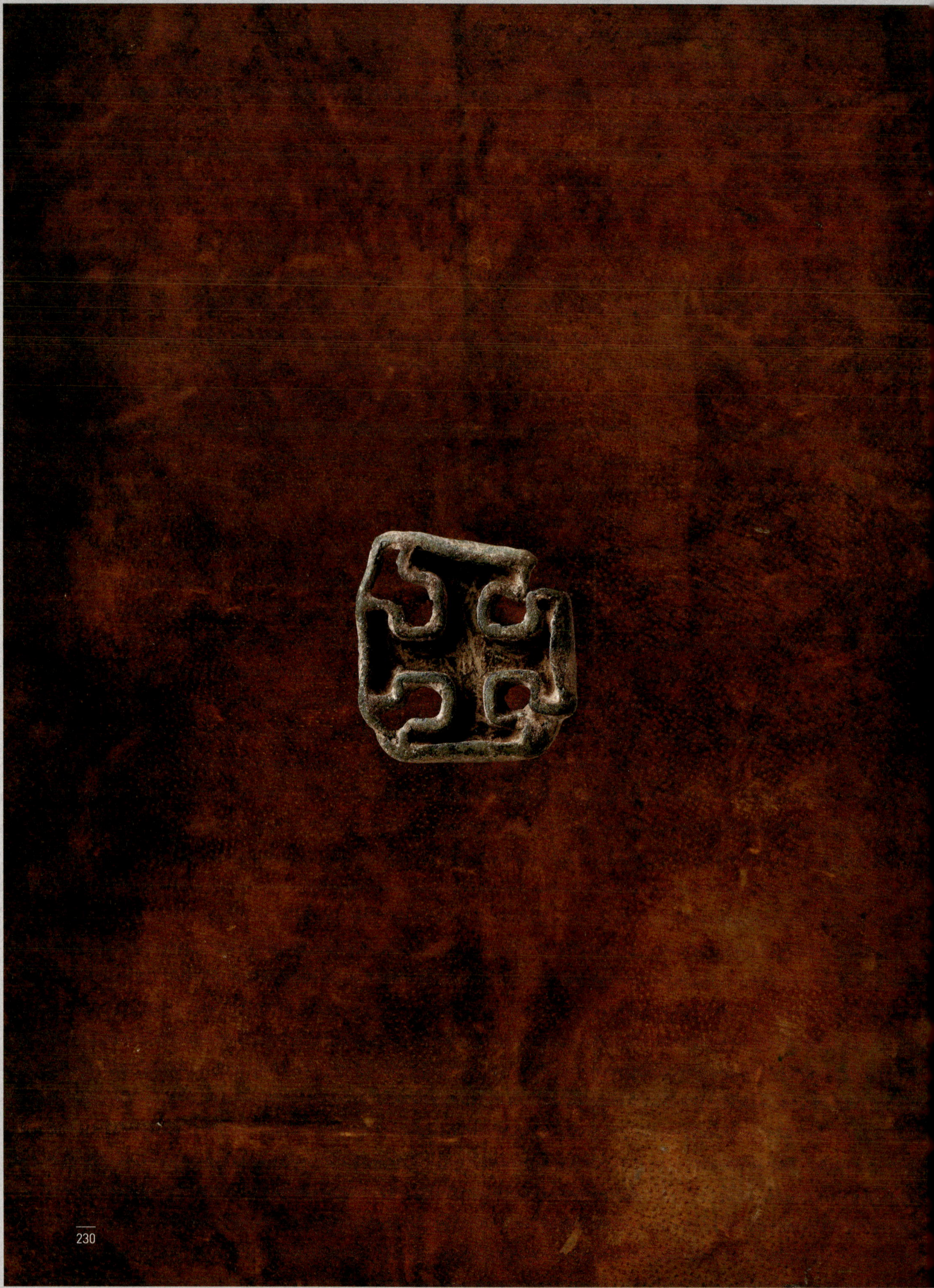

阿克瑟斯文明 Oxus Civilization

363

| 题材 Subject Matter |
| 铭文 Inscription |

| 阿克瑟斯文明 Oxus Civilization | 364-365 | 题材 Subject Matter |
| | | 铭文 Inscription |

364

365

阿克瑟斯文明 Oxus Civilization

366-367

| 题材 Subject Matter |
| 几何纹 Geometry Pattern |

366

367

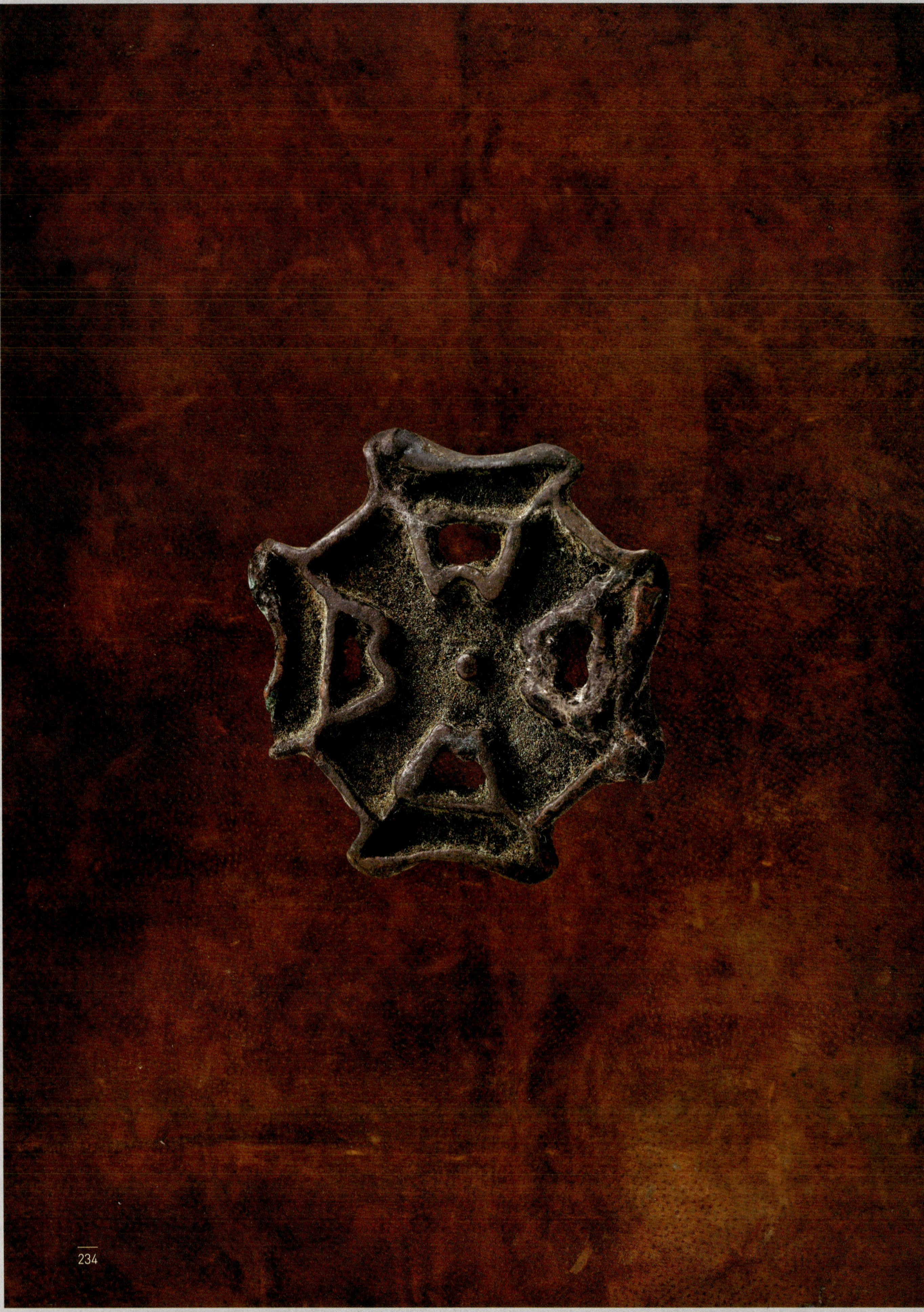

| 阿克瑟斯文明 Oxus Civilization | 368-369 | 题材 Subject Matter |
| | | 几何纹 Geometry Pattern |

368

369

阿克瑟斯文明 Oxus Civilization 370-371

| 题材 |
| Subject Matter |

| 铭文 |
| Inscription |

370

371

阿克瑟斯文明 Oxus Civilization

372

题材 Subject Matter
几何纹 Geometry Pattern

372

| 阿克瑟斯文明 Oxus Civilization | 373-374 | 题材 Subject Matter |
| | | 几何纹 Geometry Pattern |

373

374

阿克瑟斯文明　Oxus Civilization	375-376	题材　Subject Matter
		几何纹　Geometry Pattern

375

376

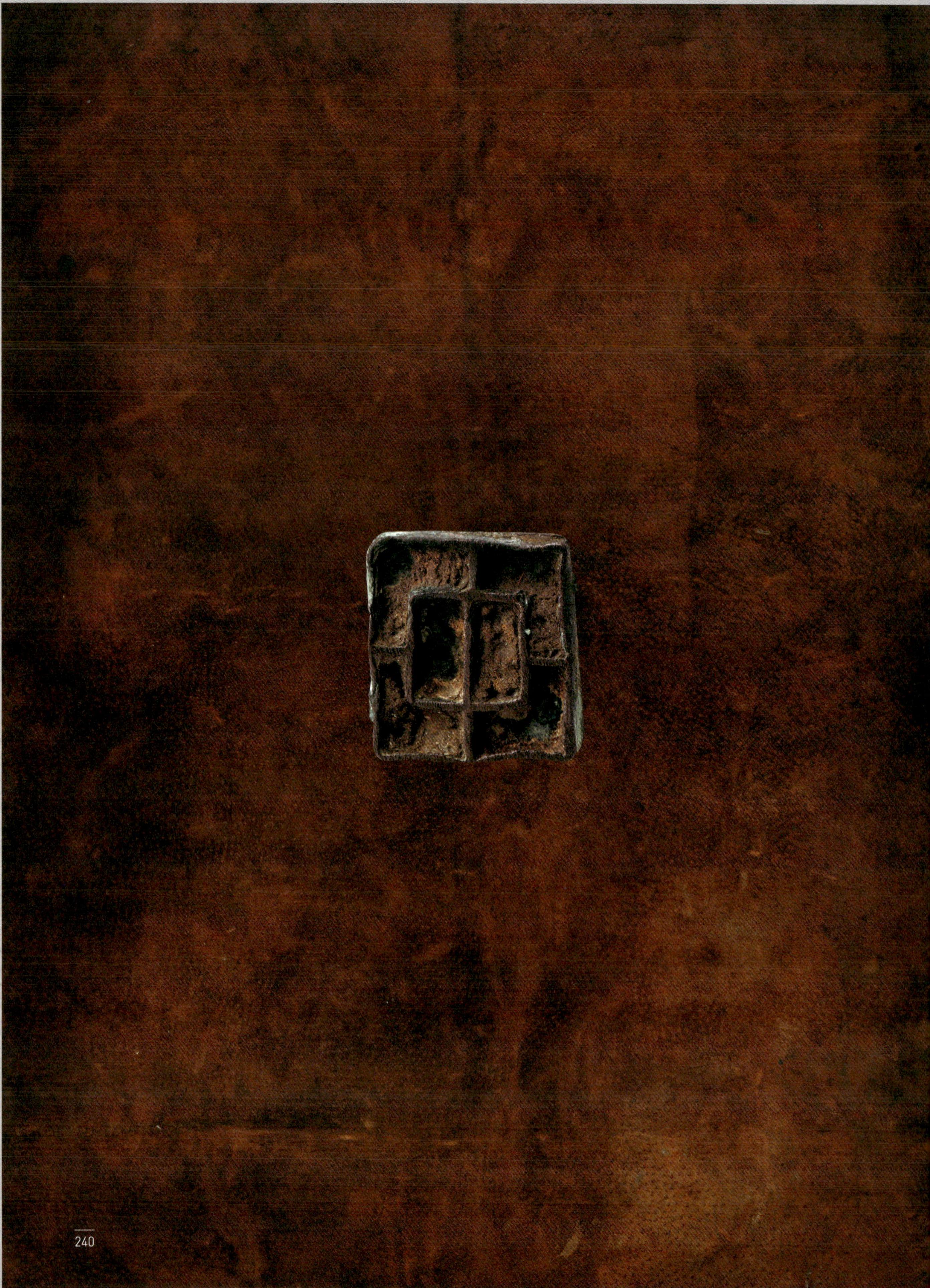

阿克瑟斯文明　Oxus Civilization 377

题材　Subject Matter

铭文　Inscription

377

阿克瑟斯文明 Oxus Civilization

378-382

| 题材 Subject Matter |
| 铭文 Inscription |

378　　379　　380　　381　　382

阿克瑟斯文明 Oxus Civilization 383-386

题材
Subject Matter

铭文
Inscription

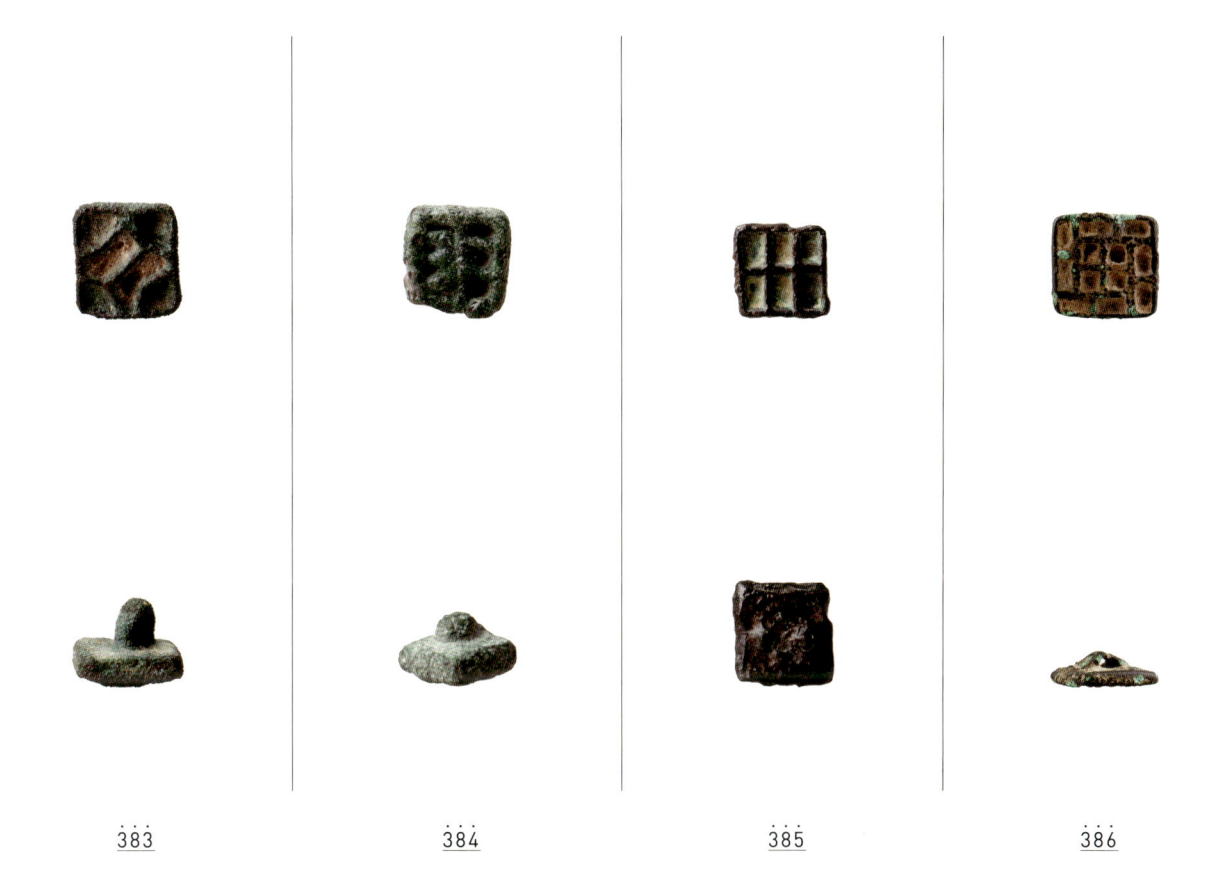

383

384

385

386

阿克瑟斯文明　Oxus Civilization	387-389	题材　Subject Matter
		几何纹　Geometry Pattern

387

388

389

| 阿克瑟斯文明 Oxus Civilization | 390-391 | 题材 Subject Matter |
| | | 几何纹 Geometry Pattern |

390

391

阿克瑟斯文明 Oxus Civilization   392-393

题材
Subject Matter

几何纹
Geometry Pattern

392

393

阿克瑟斯文明 Oxus Civilization

394

题材
Subject Matter

几何纹
Geometry Pattern

394

| 阿克瑟斯文明 Oxus Civilization | 395-396 | 题材 Subject Matter |
| | | 几何纹 Geometry Pattern |

395

396

阿克瑟斯文明 Oxus Civilization 　　397-398

| 题材
Subject Matter

| 几何纹
Geometry Pattern

397

398

249

阿克瑟斯文明 Oxus Civilization　　399-400

题材
Subject Matter

几何纹
Geometry Pattern

399

400

阿克瑟斯文明 Oxus Civilization   401-402

| 题材
| Subject Matter
|
| 几何纹
| Geometry Pattern

401

402

251

| 阿克瑟斯文明 Oxus Civilization | 403-404 | 题材 Subject Matter |
| | | 几何纹 Geometry Pattern |

403

404

阿克瑟斯文明 Oxus Civilization

405-406

题材
Subject Matter

几何纹
Geometry Pattern

405

406

| 阿克瑟斯文明 Oxus Civilization | 407-408 | 题材 Subject Matter |
| | | 几何纹 Geometry Pattern |

407

408

| 阿克瑟斯文明 Oxus Civilization | 409-410 | 题材 Subject Matter |
| | | 几何纹 Geometry Pattern |

409

410

阿克瑟斯文明　Oxus Civilization

411

题材
Subject Matter

几何纹
Geometry Pattern

411

阿克瑟斯文明 Oxus Civilization	412-413	题材 Subject Matter
		几何纹 Geometry Pattern

412

413

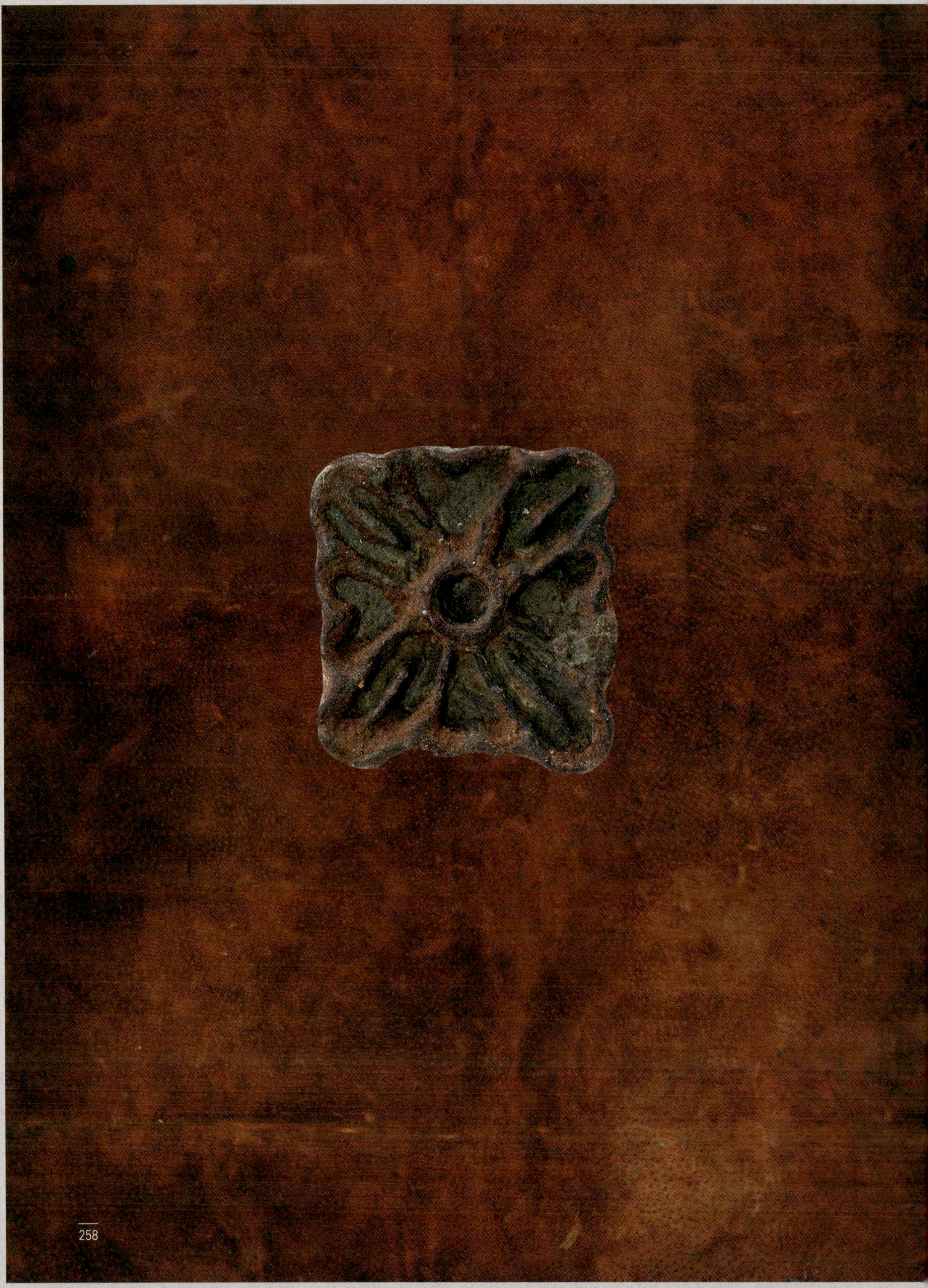

阿克瑟斯文明 Oxus Civilization 414

题材 Subject Matter
植物 Plant

414

阿克瑟斯文明　Oxus Civilization

415

题材
Subject Matter

几何纹
Geometry Pattern

415

阿克瑟斯文明　Oxus Civilization

416

题材
Subject Matter

几何纹
Geometry Pattern

416

261

阿克瑟斯文明 Oxus Civilization

索引表
INDEX

页码	顺序	总账号	分类号	质料	测量方法	规格 (mm)
005	001	XC11651	YZ5669	铜	直径 × 印章高度	57.21×15.17
006	002	XC11562	YZ5580	铜	直径 × 印章高度	47.79×17.43
007	003	XC11473	YZ5491	铜	直径 × 印章高度	29.58×14.41
008	004	XC11611	YZ5629	铜	长 × 宽 × 印章高度	49.31×48.62×20.19
009	005	XC11662	YZ5680	铜	直径 × 印章高度	71.34×18.42
011	006	XC11441	YZ5459	铜	长 × 宽 × 印章高度	21.77×23.73×11.26
012	007	XC11334	YZ5352	铜	底 × 高 × 印章高度	16.73×30.77×7.59
012	008	XC11298	YZ5316	铜	底 × 高 × 印章高度	17.72×27.28×11.83
012	009	XC11230	YZ5248	铜	长 × 宽 × 印章高度	23.70×10.35×9.11
013	010	XC11283	YZ5301	铜	长 × 宽 × 印章高度	23.60×13.85×19.04
013	011	XC11464	YZ5482	铜	长 × 宽 × 印章高度	27.28×10.47×12.60
013	012	XC11338	YZ5356	铜	底 × 高 × 印章高度	16.24×31.29×12.28
015	013	XC11554	YZ5572	铜	直径 × 印章高度	48.75×15.42
015	014	XC11504	YZ5522	铜	直径 × 印章高度	37.78×12.70
016	015	XC11233	YZ5251	铜	直径 × 印章高度	20.69×11.62
016	016	XC11587	YZ5605	铜	十字线 1× 十字线 2× 印章高度	36.49×30.89×15.21
016	017	XC11260	YZ5278	铜	底 × 高 × 印章高度	21.98×16.29×8.01
017	018	XC11569	YZ5587	铜	底 × 高 × 印章高度	40.24×48.25×16.79
018	019	XC11439	YZ5457	铜	底 × 高 × 印章高度	25.39×21.64×15.42
018	020	XC11408	YZ5426	铜	长 × 宽 × 印章高度	17.94×16.26×7.26
018	021	XC11304	YZ5322	铜	直径 × 印章高度	20.99×26.33
019	022	XC11513	YZ5531	铜	十字线 1× 十字线 2× 印章高度	48.63×37.06×8.29
020	023	XC11565	YZ5583	铜	直径 × 印章高度	46.29×18.69
020	024	XC11647	YZ5665	铜	直径 × 印章高度	59.21×19.68
021	025	XC11593	YZ5611	铜	长 × 宽 × 印章高度	36.92×35.36×14.36
022	026	XC11656	YZ5674	铜	直径 × 印章高度	64.11×19.20
023	027	XC11650	YZ5668	铜	直径 × 印章高度	11.94×16.76
025	028	XC11489	YZ5507	铜	长 × 宽 × 印章高度	34.23×32.92×9.51

续表
CONTINUE THE TABLE

页码	顺序	总账号	分类号	质料	测量方法	规格 (mm)
026	029	XC11493	YZ5511	铜	直径 × 印章高度	34.88×11.55
026	030	XC11589	YZ5607	铜	长轴 × 短轴 × 印章高度	39.09×33.98×17.27
027	031	XC11258	YZ5276	铜	直径 × 印章高度	16.54×10.56
027	032	XC11457	YZ5475	铜	直径 × 印章高度	28.99×9.50
029	033	XC11412	YZ5430	铜	长 × 宽 × 印章高度	18.29×18.32×7.48
030	034	XC11219	YZ5237	铜	直径 × 印章高度	23.71×6.11
031	035	XC11218	YZ5236	铜	直径 × 印章高度	23.70×5.88
032	036	XC11322	YZ5340	铜	底 × 高 × 印章高度	26.94×227.31×9.72
033	037	XC11326	YZ5344	铜	长 × 宽 × 印章高度	30.15×25.38×4.80
035	038	XC11600	YZ5618	铜	直径 × 印章高度	45.68×15.28
036	039	XC11597	YZ5615	铜	直径 × 印章高度	43.04×18.45
037	040	XC11612	YZ5630	铜	直径 × 印章高度	49.60×17.41
037	041	XC11614	YZ5632	铜	直径 × 印章高度	49.73×25.73
038	042	XC11582	YZ5600	铜	长 × 宽 × 印章高度	25.16×39.22×9.03
039	043	XC11468	YZ5486	铜	长 × 宽 × 印章高度	24,90×13.30×27.68
039	044	XC11588	YZ5606	铜	长 × 宽 × 印章高度	40.65×29.08×33.92
041	045	XC11598	YZ5616	铜	长轴 × 短轴 × 印章高度	42.00×31.10×18.24
042	046	XC11500	YZ5518	铜	直径 × 印章高度	45.59×17.04
043	047	XC11581	YZ5599	铜	长 × 宽 × 印章高度	38.23×24.71×11.11
044	048	XC11345	YZ5363	铜	长 × 宽 × 印章高度	32.07×29.57×16.34
045	049	XC11395	YZ5413	铜	长 × 宽 × 印章高度	16.93×16.40×8.54
045	050	XC11403	YZ5421	铜	长 × 宽 × 印章高度	17.48×17.74×9.08
046	051	XC11377	YZ5395	铜	长 × 宽 × 印章高度	15.08×15.08×6.12
047	052	XC11579	YZ5597	铜	长 × 宽 × 印章高度	36.62×22.71×10.09
048	053	XC11605	YZ5623	铜	长 × 宽 × 印章高度	43.28×22.88×30.80
048	054	XC11339	YZ5357	铜	长 × 宽 × 印章高度	34.92×22.23×24.98
049	055	XC11461	YZ5479	铜	直径 × 印章高度	27.89×11.94
049	056	XC11648	YZ5666	铜	底 × 高 × 印章高度	59.28×45.66×16.59
050	057	XC11570	YZ5588	铜	长 × 宽 × 印章高度	41.48×40.73×9.21
051	058	XC11481	YZ5499	铜	长 × 宽 × 印章高度	33.38×23.80×16.85
051	059	XC11474	YZ5492	铜	长 × 宽 × 印章高度	32.17×28.85×8.49
051	060	XC11483	YZ5501	铜	长 × 宽 × 印章高度	33.83×23.33×10.45
052	061	XC11456	YZ5474	铜	直径 × 印章高度	26.70×8.94
052	062	XC11586	YZ5604	铜	长 × 宽 × 印章高度	35.73×30.01×8.99

续表
CONTINUE THE TABLE

页码	顺序	总账号	分类号	质料	测量方法	规格 (mm)
053	063	XC11573	YZ5591	铜	直径 × 印章高度	43.73×14.80
053	064	XC11264	YZ5282	铜	直径 × 印章高度	23.59×16.97
054	065	XC11601	YZ5619	铜	直径 × 印章高度	44.43×14.97
055	066	XC11602	YZ5620	铜	直径 × 印章高度	47.52×14.41
057	067	XC11621	YZ5639	铜	直径 × 印章高度	50.94×18.42
058	068	XC11666	YZ5684	铜	长 × 宽 × 印章高度	58.52×54.16×17.40
059	069	XC11653	YZ5671	铜	长 × 宽 × 印章高度	61.36×40.78×25.71
061	070	XC11285	YZ5303	铜	直径 × 印章高度	19.28×25.03
061	071	XC11291	YZ5309	铜	直径 × 印章高度	15.60×27.57
061	072	XC11245	YZ5263	铜	直径 × 印章高度	13.10×24.27
061	073	XC11328	YZ5346	铜	直径 × 印章高度	14.76×30.23
061	074	XC11229	YZ5247	铜	直径 × 印章高度	10.20×22.20
061	075	XC11247	YZ5265	铜	直径 × 印章高度	13.63×18.84
061	076	XC11416	YZ5434	铜	直径 × 印章高度	18.53×10.39
061	077	XC11246	YZ5264	铜	直径 × 印章高度	13.53×23.41
061	078	XC11257	YZ5275	铜	直径 × 印章高度	15.89×24.77
061	079	XC11361	YZ5379	铜	直径 × 印章高度	12.41×13.05
062	080	XC11348	YZ5366	铜	长 × 宽 × 印章高度	10.17×10.29×5.69
062	081	XC11347	YZ5365	铜	长 × 宽 × 印章高度	8.87×9.64×5.90
062	082	XC11352	YZ5370	铜	长 × 宽 × 印章高度	11.59×11.49×8.10
062	083	XC11355	YZ5373	铜	长 × 宽 × 印章高度	11.92×11.84×7.88
062	084	XC11351	YZ5369	铜	长 × 宽 × 印章高度	9.41×11.24×10.28
063	085	XC11417	YZ5435	铜	直径 × 印章高度	18.76×12.62
063	086	XC11428	YZ5446	铜	长 × 宽 × 印章高度	22.07×20.83×12.21
065	087	XC11576	YZ5594	铜	直径 × 印章高度	39.70×18.93
066	088	XC11240	YZ5258	铜	直径 × 印章高度	19.57×12.41
066	089	XC11438	YZ5456	铜	直径 × 印章高度	21.64×22.18
066	090	XC11466	YZ5484	铜	直径 × 印章高度	26.16×12.75
067	091	XC11639	YZ5657	铜	直径 × 印章高度	45.74×17.26
067	092	XC11655	YZ5673	铜	直径 × 印章高度	62.69×20.32
069	093	XC11633	YZ5651	铜	直径 × 印章高度	53.77×13.02
070	094	XC11225	YZ5243	铜	直径 × 印章高度	23.36×9.44
071	095	XC11325	YZ5343	铜	直径 × 印章高度	29.85×10.47
072	096	XC11514	YZ5532	铜	直径 × 印章高度	39.10×15.70

续表
CONTINUE THE TABLE

页码	顺序	总账号	分类号	质料	测量方法	规格 (mm)
072	097	XC11505	YZ5523	铜	直径 × 印章高度	39.92×12.89
073	098	XC11631	YZ5649	铜	直径 × 印章高度	52.73×16.20
074	099	XC11546	YZ5564	铜	直径 × 印章高度	46.11×13.12
074	100	XC11547	YZ5565	铜	直径 × 印章高度	46.53×10.70
075	101	XC11652	YZ5670	铜	直径 × 印章高度	61.27×16.27
076	102	XC11627	YZ5645	铜	直径 × 印章高度	52.21×14.42
077	103	XC11637	YZ5655	铜	直径 × 印章高度	45.51×12.96
077	104	XC11574	YZ5592	铜	直径 × 印章高度	35.55×17.37
078	105	XC11629	YZ5647	铜	直径 × 印章高度	52.33×15.52
079	106	XC11608	YZ5626	铜	直径 × 印章高度	54.92×23.01
080	107	XC11620	YZ5638	铜	直径 × 印章高度	54.33×17.30
081	108	XC11566	YZ5584	铜	直径 × 印章高度	48.67×23.23
082	109	XC11649	YZ5667	铜	直径 × 印章高度	58.38×23.94
083	110	XC11663	YZ5681	铜	直径 × 印章高度	71.73×21.20
084	111	XC11640	YZ5658	铜	长 × 宽 × 印章高度	42.51×39.31×13.78
085	112	XC11624	YZ5642	铜	直径 × 印章高度	51.13×11.97
087	113	XC11488	YZ5506	铜	长 × 宽 × 印章高度	34.09×32.17×17.52
088	114	XC11359	YZ5377	铜	长 × 宽 × 印章高度	12.33×11.90×7.91
088	115	XC11360	YZ5378	铜	长 × 宽 × 印章高度	12.58×12.64×9.63
088	116	XC11353	YZ5371	铜	长 × 宽 × 印章高度	11.66×10.33×5.52
088	117	XC11434	YZ5452	铜	长 × 宽 × 印章高度	21.60×21.35×11.11
089	118	XC11356	YZ5374	铜	长 × 宽 × 印章高度	12.72×11.42×6.78
089	119	XC11410	YZ5428	铜	长 × 宽 × 印章高度	18.19×18.09×10.40
089	120	XC11405	YZ5423	铜	十字线 1× 十字线 2× 印章高度	17.77×17.81×9.79
091	121	XC11315	YZ5333	铜	直径 × 印章高度	29.25×25.77
092	122	XC11227	YZ5245	铜	直径 × 印章高度	19.24×9.55
092	123	XC11238	YZ5256	铜	直径 × 印章高度	21.57×12.31
092	124	XC11301	YZ5319	铜	直径 × 印章高度	26.20×5.56
093	125	XC11254	YZ5272	铜	直径 × 印章高度	23.42×15.10
093	126	XC11221	YZ5239	铜	直径 × 印章高度	22.65×6.97
094	127	XC11223	YZ5241	铜	直径 × 印章高度	22.63×7.66
094	128	XC11455	YZ5473	铜	直径 × 印章高度	27.26×8.71
095	129	XC11616	YZ5634	铜	直径 × 印章高度	21.69×49.87
097	130	XC11318	YZ5336	铜	长 × 宽 × 印章高度	27.75×25.97×18.34

续表
CONTINUE THE TABLE

页码	顺序	总账号	分类号	质料	测量方法	规格 (mm)
098	131	XC11350	YZ5368	铜	长 × 宽 × 印章高度	11.03×11.03×4.02
098	132	XC11280	YZ5298	铜	长 × 宽 × 印章高度	22.74×18.62×12.42
099	133	XC11433	YZ5451	铜	长 × 宽 × 印章高度	23.94×21.21×13.47
099	134	XC11343	YZ5361	铜	长 × 宽 × 印章高度	31.93×30.14×18.39
100	135	XC11506	YZ5524	铜	直径 × 印章高度	39.23×13.23
101	136	XC11332	YZ5350	铜	长 × 宽 × 印章高度	30.58×29.44×14.35
103	137	XC11609	YZ5627	铜	长 × 宽 × 印章高度	45.84×46.30×24.05
104	138	XC11386	YZ5404	铜	十字线1× 十字线2× 印章高度	15.68×15.55×6.59
105	139	XC11419	YZ5437	铜	十字线1× 十字线2× 印章高度	22.54×19.97×9.87
106	140	XC11389	YZ5407	铜	十字线1× 十字线2× 印章高度	16.22×15.88×8.21
106	141	XC11448	YZ5466	铜	十字线1× 十字线2× 印章高度	24.23×23.55×14.07
106	142	XC11368	YZ5386	铜	十字线1× 十字线2× 印章高度	14.00×13.91×4.10
107	143	XC11330	YZ5348	铜	直径 × 印章高度	30.35×9.16
108	144	XC11606	YZ5624	铜	长 × 宽 × 印章高度	46.21×43.13×20.85
109	145	XC11622	YZ5640	铜	底 × 高 × 印章高度	51.04×35.48×22.40
111	146	XC11591	YZ5609	铜	长 × 宽 × 印章高度	34.76×35.59×15.79
112	147	XC11444	YZ5462	铜	十字线1× 十字线2× 印章高度	24.00×21.92×10.62
112	148	XC11316	YZ5334	铜	十字线1× 十字线2× 印章高度	27.28×25.86×9.94
112	149	XC11423	YZ5441	铜	长 × 宽 × 印章高度	21.47×20.37×8.68
113	150	XC11567	YZ5585	铜	十字线1× 十字线2× 印章高度	40.81×40.74×15.36
113	151	XC11568	YZ5586	铜	长 × 宽 × 印章高度	42.36×42.08×20.31
114	152	XC11317	YZ5335	铜	十字线1× 十字线2× 印章高度	26.15×25.89×11.67
114	153	XC11342	YZ5360	铜	十字线1× 十字线2× 印章高度	31.82×30.70×15.08
114	154	XC11313	YZ5331	铜	十字线1× 十字线2× 印章高度	26.52×25.54×10.07
115	155	XC11369	YZ5387	铜	长 × 宽 × 印章高度	14.07×13.56×4.77
115	156	XC11424	YZ5442	铜	十字线1× 十字线2× 印章高度	20.40×20.40×8.29
115	157	XC11388	YZ5406	铜	十字线1× 十字线2× 印章高度	15.92×15.28×4.62
116	158	XC11321	YZ5339	铜	长 × 宽 × 印章高度	27.36×26.79×14.35
116	159	XC11310	YZ5328	铜	长 × 宽 × 印章高度	24.48×26.59×14.00
116	160	XC11421	YZ5439	铜	长 × 宽 × 印章高度	20.14×20.43×11.14
117	161	XC11374	YZ5392	铜	长 × 宽 × 印章高度	14.69×14.47×8.17
117	162	XC11349	YZ5367	铜	长 × 宽 × 印章高度	10.63×11.01×4.00
117	163	XC11400	YZ5418	铜	长 × 宽 × 印章高度	17.41×16.58×10.41
117	164	XC11358	YZ5376	铜	长 × 宽 × 印章高度	12.31×12.33×6.31

续表
CONTINUE THE TABLE

页码	顺序	总账号	分类号	质料	测量方法	规格 (mm)
117	165	XC11284	YZ5302	铜	长 × 宽 × 印章高度	19.05×19.53×9.88
118	166	XC11426	YZ5444	铜	长 × 宽 × 印章高度	25.71×24.48×9.19
118	167	XC11450	YZ5468	铜	十字线 1× 十字线 2× 印章高度	25.27×24.44×10.36
118	168	XC11314	YZ5332	铜	长 × 宽 × 印章高度	25.85×25.72×13.28
119	169	XC11235	YZ5253	铜	直径 × 印章高度	21.30×12.05
121	170	XC11615	YZ5633	铜	长 × 宽 × 印章高度	49.86×49.48×21.24
122	171	XC11636	YZ5654	铜	直径 × 印章高度	45.01×17.89
122	172	XC11509	YZ5527	铜	直径 × 印章高度	40.21×13.65
123	173	XC11642	YZ5660	铜	直径 × 印章高度	43.59×19.40
124	174	XC11337	YZ5355	铜	长 × 宽 × 印章高度	31.18×30.77×22.52
124	175	XC11596	YZ5614	铜	长 × 宽 × 印章高度	37.00×35.89×15.19
125	176	XC11623	YZ5641	铜	直径 × 印章高度	51.11×15.01
125	177	XC11510	YZ5528	铜	直径 × 印章高度	39.92×13.81
126	178	XC11564	YZ5582	铜	直径 × 印章高度	48.84×18.16
127	179	XC11669	YZ5687	铜	直径 × 印章高度	67.36×25.34
128	180	XC11660	YZ5678	铜	直径 × 印章高度	67.89×13.57
129	181	XC11327	YZ5345	铜	长 × 宽 × 印章高度	29.66×30.17×23.33
129	182	XC11572	YZ5590	铜	直径 × 印章高度	35.91×16.77
131	183	XC11503	YZ5521	铜	直径 × 印章高度	38.61×12.60
132	184	XC11479	YZ5497	铜	直径 × 印章高度	32.96×13.07
132	185	XC11496	YZ5514	铜	直径 × 印章高度	34.97×11.87
133	186	XC11563	YZ5581	铜	直径 × 印章高度	49.16×18.02
134	187	XC11480	YZ5498	铜	直径 × 印章高度	33.18×11.35
134	188	XC11617	YZ5635	铜	直径 × 印章高度	50.07×20.17
134	189	XC11241	YZ5259	铜	直径 × 印章高度	25.01×12.48
135	190	XC11626	YZ5644	铜	直径 × 印章高度	51.46×23.60
137	191	XC11561	YZ5579	铜	直径 × 印章高度	46.93×17.30
138	192	XC11583	YZ5601	铜	长 × 宽 × 印章高度	36.03×25.86×17.02
138	193	XC11331	YZ5349	铜	长 × 宽 × 印章高度	30.36×22.25×17.34
139	194	XC11452	YZ5470	铜	长 × 宽 × 印章高度	25.25×25.10×13.13
139	195	XC11475	YZ5493	铜	长 × 宽 × 印章高度	32.41×31.12×17.69
140	196	XC11549	YZ5567	铜	直径 × 印章高度	46.41×13.58
141	197	XC11512	YZ5530	铜	直径 × 印章高度	37.74×15.08
142	198	XC11654	YZ5672	铜	直径 × 印章高度	56.90×16.09

续表
CONTINUE THE TABLE

页码	顺序	总账号	分类号	质料	测量方法	规格 (mm)
142	199	XC11613	YZ5631	铜	直径×印章高度	49.61×19.24
143	200	XC11590	YZ5608	铜	长×宽×印章高度	34.67×36.44×15.78
145	201	XC11646	YZ5664	铜	直径×印章高度	58.76×12.65
146	202	XC11560	YZ5578	铜	直径×印章高度	46.57×17.00
146	203	XC11548	YZ5566	铜	直径×印章高度	49.52×10.95
147	204	XC11508	YZ5526	铜	直径×印章高度	37.86×13.47
149	205	XC11634	YZ5652	铜	直径×印章高度	53.89×19.59
150	206	XC11577	YZ5595	铜	长×宽×印章高度	40.91×41.50×19.20
150	207	XC11501	YZ5519	铜	长×宽×印章高度	35.48×33.38×15.30
151	208	XC11630	YZ5648	铜	直径×印章高度	52.70×8.20
152	209	XC11557	YZ5575	铜	直径×印章高度	47.14×16.70
153	210	XC11635	YZ5653	铜	直径×印章高度	54.27×13.51
154	211	XC11553	YZ5571	铜	直径×印章高度	48.68×15.04
155	212	XC11619	YZ5637	铜	直径×印章高度	50.26×13.63
157	213	XC11667	YZ5685	铜	直径×印章高度	95.15×15.54
159	214	XC11550	YZ5568	铜	直径×印章高度	49.23×13.99
160	215	XC11664	YZ5682	铜	直径×印章高度	74.26×22.71
161	216	XC11659	YZ5677	铜	直径×印章高度	67.50×15.69
162	217	XC11580	YZ5598	铜	直径×印章高度	40.32×24.29
162	218	XC11625	YZ5643	铜	直径×印章高度	51.16×14.18
163	219	XC11618	YZ5636	铜	直径×印章高度	55.53×19.02
164	220	XC11578	YZ5596	铜	直径×印章高度	38.71×19.79
165	221	XC11657	YZ5675	铜	直径×印章高度	57.34×18.53
166	222	XC11465	YZ5483	铜	直径×印章高度	28.83×12.63
167	223	XC11645	YZ5663	铜	直径×印章高度	41.32×7.20
169	224	XC11638	YZ5656	铜	长×宽×印章高度	43.84×40.56×15.32
170	225	XC11248	YZ5266	铜	直径×印章高度	23.91×13.66
170	226	XC11470	YZ5488	铜	直径×印章高度	26.52×14.20
170	227	XC11365	YZ5383	铜	直径×印章高度	13.74×7.02
171	228	XC11399	YZ5417	铜	直径×印章高度	17.29×8.50
171	229	XC11378	YZ5396	铜	直径×印章高度	15.13×11.76
172	230	XC11294	YZ5312	铜	直径×印章高度	26.39×16.61
172	231	XC11538	YZ5556	铜	直径×印章高度	20.84×16.45
173	232	XC11222	YZ5240	铜	直径×印章高度	20.66×7.08

续表
CONTINUE THE TABLE

页码	顺序	总账号	分类号	质料	测量方法	规格 (mm)
173	233	XC11346	YZ5364	铜	直径×印章高度	9.63×6.06
173	234	XC11406	YZ5424	铜	直径×印章高度	17.85×8.58
173	235	XC11320	YZ5338	铜	直径×印章高度	24.09×9.74
173	236	XC11370	YZ5388	铜	直径×印章高度	14.17×7.49
173	237	XC11364	YZ5382	铜	直径×印章高度	13.71×7.84
173	238	XC11373	YZ5391	铜	直径×印章高度	14.49×7.78
173	239	XC11460	YZ5478	铜	直径×印章高度	26.26×11.72
173	240	XC11453	YZ5471	铜	直径×印章高度	26.19×7.48
174	241	XC11226	YZ5244	铜	直径×印章高度	19.30×9.45
174	242	XC11228	YZ5246	铜	直径×印章高度	22.01×9.67
174	243	XC11234	YZ5252	铜	直径×印章高度	23.18×11.78
174	244	XC11274	YZ5292	铜	直径×印章高度	22.64×11.20
174	245	XC11266	YZ5284	铜	直径×印章高度	28.38×11.39
175	246	XC11239	YZ5257	铜	直径×印章高度	21.09×12.37
175	247	XC11401	YZ5419	铜	直径×印章高度	17.54×8.73
175	248	XC11231	YZ5249	铜	直径×印章高度	20.05×10.77
175	249	XC11404	YZ5422	铜	直径×印章高度	17.75×8.40
176	250	XC11502	YZ5520	铜	直径×印章高度	37.24×11.46
177	251	XC11335	YZ5353	铜	直径×印章高度	30.97×12.91
177	252	XC11551	YZ5569	铜	直径×印章高度	48.07×14.34
179	253	XC11290	YZ5308	铜	直径×印章高度	14.57×27.27
180	254	XC11391	YZ5409	铜	直径×印章高度	11.94×16.76
180	255	XC11467	YZ5485	铜	直径×印章高度	12.96×28.95
180	256	XC11382	YZ5400	铜	直径×印章高度	15.33×15.38
181	257	XC11253	YZ5271	铜	直径×印章高度	14.99×23.70
181	258	XC11236	YZ5254	铜	直径×印章高度	12.10×25.31
181	259	XC11471	YZ5489	铜	直径×印章高度	14.28×26.88
181	260	XC11357	YZ5375	铜	直径×印章高度	10.59×12.27
181	261	XC11393	YZ5411	铜	直径×印章高度	14.54×25.75
181	262	XC11390	YZ5408	铜	直径×印章高度	16.29×11.42
181	263	XC11293	YZ5311	铜	直径×印章高度	16.41×27.48
181	264	XC11292	YZ5310	铜	直径×印章高度	15.86×26.78
181	265	XC11463	YZ5481	铜	直径×印章高度	12.57×27.90
182	266	XC11268	YZ5286	铜	直径×印章高度	17.74×19.10

续表
CONTINUE THE TABLE

页码	顺序	总账号	分类号	质料	测量方法	规格 (mm)
182	267	XC11276	YZ5294	铜	直径×印章高度	19.94×18.15
182	268	XC11220	YZ5238	铜	直径×印章高度	21.94×6.69
183	269	XC11255	YZ5273	铜	直径×印章高度	15.46×20.46
183	270	XC11265	YZ5283	铜	直径×印章高度	17.14×20.34
183	271	XC11244	YZ5262	铜	直径×印章高度	13.01×23.78
183	272	XC11243	YZ5261	铜	直径×印章高度	12.95×22.56
183	273	XC11300	YZ5318	铜	直径×印章高度	18.03×29.44
183	274	XC11250	YZ5268	铜	直径×印章高度	13.73×18.95
184	275	XC11344	YZ5362	铜	直径×印章高度	17.80×32.06
184	276	XC11427	YZ5445	铜	直径×印章高度	22.07×20.80
184	277	XC11333	YZ5351	铜	直径×印章高度	30.59×13.98
185	278	XC11443	YZ5461	铜	直径×印章高度	24.25×21.87
185	279	XC11305	YZ5323	铜	直径×印章高度	23.26×25.88
185	280	XC11447	YZ5465	铜	直径×印章高度	23.34×23.01
185	281	XC11429	YZ5447	铜	直径×印章高度	20.84×21.35
185	282	XC11341	YZ5359	铜	直径×印章高度	18.12×20.98
185	283	XC11272	YZ5290	铜	直径×印章高度	17.89×21.90
185	284	XC11273	YZ5291	铜	直径×印章高度	18.09×20.77
185	285	XC11422	YZ5440	铜	长轴×短轴×印章高度	21.81×17.34×20.20
185	286	XC11432	YZ5450	铜	直径×印章高度	21.06×22.62
187	287	XC11477	YZ5495	铜	直径×印章高度	32.74×27.46
188	288	XC11288	YZ5306	铜	直径×印章高度	12.34×23.86
188	289	XC11249	YZ5267	铜	直径×印章高度	13.68×19.89
189	290	XC11485	YZ5503	铜	直径×印章高度	17.23×33.78
189	291	XC11232	YZ5250	铜	直径×印章高度	11.25×22.96
190	292	XC11415	YZ5433	铜	直径×印章高度	18.51×9.55
190	293	XC11788	YZ5806	铜	直径×印章高度	31.13×27.87
191	294	XC11472	YZ5490	铜	直径×印章高度	25.71×14.32
191	295	XC11498	YZ5516	铜	直径×印章高度	35.33×29.35
192	296	XC11282	YZ5300	铜	直径×印章高度	19.04×22.03
192	297	XC11306	YZ5324	铜	长轴×短轴×印章高度	23.28×18.98×26.75
192	298	XC11437	YZ5455	铜	直径×印章高度	21.59×25.30
192	299	XC11269	YZ5287	铜	直径×印章高度	20.62×17.78
193	300	XC11449	YZ5467	铜	底×高×印章高度	24.67×20.97×24.33

续表
CONTINUE THE TABLE

页码	顺序	总账号	分类号	质料	测量方法	规格 (mm)
193	301	XC11397	YZ5415	铜	直径×印章高度	17.20×15.31
193	302	XC11435	YZ5453	铜	直径×印章高度	25.63×21.44
194	303	XC11270	YZ5288	铜	直径×印章高度	20.37×17.85
194	304	XC11277	YZ5295	铜	直径×印章高度	21.71×18.55
195	305	XC11420	YZ5438	铜	直径×印章高度	27.58×29.70
195	306	XC11237	YZ5255	铜	直径×印章高度	19.90×12.13
196	307	XC11585	YZ5603	铜	直径×印章高度	29.97×37.68
197	308	XC11319	YZ5337	铜	直径×印章高度	29.39×25.97
198	309	XC11278	YZ5296	铜	直径×印章高度	18.58×20.61
198	310	XC11287	YZ5305	铜	直径×印章高度	22.30×19.64
198	311	XC11252	YZ5270	铜	直径×印章高度	24.36×14.01
199	312	XC11329	YZ5347	铜	长轴×短轴×印章高度	21.26×17.55×30.27
199	313	XC11379	YZ5397	铜	直径×印章高度	15.17×11.08
199	314	XC11340	YZ5358	铜	直径×印章高度	16.88×27.14
199	315	XC11324	YZ5342	铜	直径×印章高度	18.09×32.21
199	316	XC11366	YZ5384	铜	长轴×短轴×印章高度	13.80×10.64×13.58
200	317	XC11469	YZ5487	铜	直径×印章高度	13.54×28.04
200	318	XC11286	YZ5304	铜	直径×印章高度	19.28×25.45
200	319	XC11402	YZ5420	铜	直径×印章高度	14.97×17.57
200	320	XC11372	YZ5390	铜	直径×印章高度	14.32×9.08
201	321	XC11308	YZ5326	铜	底×高×印章高度	20.68×28.59×23.75
201	322	XC11307	YZ5325	铜	底×高×印章高度	16.33×26.82×23.68
203	323	XC11486	YZ5504	铜	直径×印章高度	29.78×34.01
204	324	XC11478	YZ5496	铜	直径×印章高度	32.77×21.15
205	325	XC11552	YZ5570	铜	直径×印章高度	42.82×28.14
207	326	XC11462	YZ5480	铜	长×宽×印章高度	26.57×12.48×12.43
208	327	XC11414	YZ5432	铜	直径×印章高度	15.53×18.50
208	328	XC11363	YZ5381	铜	直径×印章高度	12.99×13.49
209	329	XC11299	YZ5317	铜	直径×印章高度	17.81×27.69
209	330	XC11224	YZ5242	铜	直径×印章高度	21.47×8.25
211	331	XC11296	YZ5314	铜	直径×印章高度	26.26×17.32
212	332	XC11497	YZ5515	铜	长×宽×印章高度	35.14×34.90×16.75
212	333	XC11289	YZ5307	铜	直径×印章高度	19.90×20.37
213	334	XC11571	YZ5589	铜	长×宽×印章高度	36.27×16.53×12.90

续表
CONTINUE THE TABLE

页码	顺序	总账号	分类号	质料	测量方法	规格 (mm)
213	335	XC11584	YZ5602	铜	长 × 宽 × 印章高度	36.37×26.00×25.13
214	336	XC11411	YZ5429	铜	底 × 高 × 印章高度	18.26×17.39×11.23
214	337	XC11381	YZ5399	铜	十字线1× 十字线2× 印章高度	15.33×14.68×8.21
214	338	XC11354	YZ5372	铜	长 × 宽 × 印章高度	11.32×11.91×8.77
215	339	XC11555	YZ5573	铜	直径 × 印章高度	47.67×15.79
216	340	XC11375	YZ5393	铜	长 × 宽 × 印章高度	14.44×14.76×9.67
216	341	XC11398	YZ5416	铜	长 × 宽 × 印章高度	17.22×15.86×5.80
217	342	XC11490	YZ5508	铜	直径 × 印章高度	34.37×13.77
217	343	XC11454	YZ5472	铜	直径 × 印章高度	27.02×8.12
217	344	XC11297	YZ5315	铜	直径 × 印章高度	29.46×17.42
219	345	XC11442	YZ5460	铜	底 × 高 × 印章高度	21.86×20.79×25.57
220	346	XC11275	YZ5293	铜	底 × 高 × 印章高度	18.12×15.98×20.80
220	347	XC11323	YZ5341	铜	底 × 高 × 印章高度	27.49×26.99×17.49
221	348	XC11418	YZ5436	铜	底 × 高 × 印章高度	20.40×19.96×10.29
221	349	XC11484	YZ5502	铜	长 × 宽 × 印章高度	33.86×28.06×20.67
221	350	XC11425	YZ5443	铜	底 × 高 × 印章高度	22.92×20.70×7.02
223	351	XC11295	YZ5313	铜	长 × 宽 × 印章高度	26.03×16.73×11.08
224	352	XC11251	YZ5269	铜	底 × 高 × 印章高度	19.10×13.88×10.26
224	353	XC11392	YZ5410	铜	底 × 高 × 印章高度	16.78×10.39×7.49
224	354	XC11263	YZ5281	铜	底 × 高 × 印章高度	20.85×16.70×9.98
224	355	XC11267	YZ5285	铜	底 × 高 × 印章高度	20.59×17.67×12.28
224	356	XC11259	YZ5277	铜	底 × 高 × 印章高度	24.04×16.19×9.29
225	357	XC11279	YZ5297	铜	底 × 高 × 印章高度	21.58×18.59×10.24
225	358	XC11262	YZ5280	铜	底 × 高 × 印章高度	19.20×16.48×11.43
227	359	XC11592	YZ5610	铜	长 × 宽 × 印章高度	37.30×34.77×23.74
228	360	XC11436	YZ5454	铜	长 × 宽 × 印章高度	24.42×21.59×13.32
229	361	XC11271	YZ5289	铜	底 × 高 × 印章高度	17.87×22.15×6.98
229	362	XC11256	YZ5274	铜	长 × 宽 × 印章高度	21.54×14.65×8.59
231	363	XC11431	YZ5449	铜	长 × 宽 × 印章高度	21.61×21.03×10.80
232	364	XC11409	YZ5427	铜	直径 × 印章高度	18.03×8.70
232	365	XC11362	YZ5380	铜	十字线1× 十字线2× 印章高度	13.28×12.60×11.68
233	366	XC11371	YZ5389	铜	长 × 宽 × 印章高度	14.19×13.64×8.10
233	367	XC11396	YZ5414	铜	十字线1× 十字线2× 印章高度	17.18×17.06×7.87
235	368	XC11575	YZ5593	铜	直径 × 印章高度	38.54×17.40

续表
CONTINUE THE TABLE

页码	顺序	总账号	分类号	质料	测量方法	规格 (mm)
235	369	XC11458	YZ5476	铜	直径 × 印章高度	27.74×11.35
236	370	XC11261	YZ5279	铜	长 × 宽 × 印章高度	16.40×12.45×25.62
236	371	XC11492	YZ5510	铜	长 × 宽 × 印章高度	34.24×24.49×34.68
237	372	XC11599	YZ5617	铜	长 × 宽 × 印章高度	37.71×36.88×22.00
238	373	XC11511	YZ5529	铜	直径 × 印章高度	40.25×14.31
238	374	XC11459	YZ5477	铜	直径 × 印章高度	29.46×11.66
239	375	XC11445	YZ5463	铜	长 × 宽 × 印章高度	24.31×22.20×19.25
239	376	XC11303	YZ5321	铜	长 × 宽 × 印章高度	19.23×16.97×9.77
241	377	XC11312	YZ5330	铜	长 × 宽 × 印章高度	24.91×25.75×21.03
242	378	XC11385	YZ5403	铜	长 × 宽 × 印章高度	14.66×15.60×14.79
242	379	XC11387	YZ5405	铜	长 × 宽 × 印章高度	15.88×15.80×8.67
242	380	XC11394	YZ5412	铜	长 × 宽 × 印章高度	16.98×14.83×12.04
242	381	XC11407	YZ5425	铜	长 × 宽 × 印章高度	17.87×16.91×12.16
242	382	XC11242	YZ5260	铜	长 × 宽 × 印章高度	11.91×12.52×22.68
243	383	XC11384	YZ5402	铜	长 × 宽 × 印章高度	15.60×14.39×10.40
243	384	XC11380	YZ5398	铜	长 × 宽 × 印章高度	15.31×15.13×9.70
243	385	XC11367	YZ5385	铜	长 × 宽 × 印章高度	13.97×13.70×4.27
243	386	XC11376	YZ5394	铜	长 × 宽 × 印章高度	14.82×14.22×5.58
244	387	XC11494	YZ5512	铜	直径 × 印章高度	34.89×17.13
244	388	XC11487	YZ5505	铜	直径 × 印章高度	34.04×11.78
244	389	XC11440	YZ5458	铜	直径 × 印章高度	35.59×11.24
245	390	XC11628	YZ5646	铜	直径 × 印章高度	51.31×12.79
245	391	XC11559	YZ5577	铜	直径 × 印章高度	45.21×14.87
246	392	XC11495	YZ5513	铜	长 × 宽 × 印章高度	30.95×29.41×16.02
246	393	XC11430	YZ5448	铜	长轴 × 短轴 × 印章高度	41.95×27.84×11.32
247	394	XC11499	YZ5517	铜	直径 × 印章高度	35.40×17.58
248	395	XC11336	YZ5354	铜	长 × 宽 × 印章高度	31.04×27.31×14.63
248	396	XC11451	YZ5469	铜	长 × 宽 × 印章高度	30.16×30.76×20.91
249	397	XC11528	YZ5546	铜	长 × 宽 × 印章高度	35.46×29.86×12.35
249	398	XC11595	YZ5613	铜	底 × 高 × 印章高度	35.76×37.72×26.83
250	399	XC11604	YZ5622	铜	长 × 宽 × 印章高度	38.73×38.67×18.87
250	400	XC11661	YZ5679	铜	长 × 宽 × 印章高度	69.25×41.87×16.45
251	401	XC11482	YZ5500	铜	长 × 宽 × 印章高度	45.21×26.29×13.99
251	402	XC11603	YZ5621	铜	长 × 宽 × 印章高度	39.15×38.07×17.44

续表
CONTINUE THE TABLE

页码	顺序	总账号	分类号	质料	测量方法	规格 (mm)
252	403	XC11644	YZ5662	铜	十字线1×十字线2×印章高度	42.87×39.01×16.76
252	404	XC11643	YZ5661	铜	十字线1×十字线2×印章高度	44.60×41.66×14.32
253	405	XC11594	YZ5612	铜	长×宽×印章高度	35.68×38.26×12.95
253	406	XC11610	YZ5628	铜	长×宽×印章高度	46.56×47.10×15.28
254	407	XC11556	YZ5574	铜	直径×印章高度	47.22×16.55
254	408	XC11558	YZ5576	铜	直径×印章高度	47.12×16.90
255	409	XC11507	YZ5525	铜	直径×印章高度	39.84×13.27
255	410	XC11476	YZ5494	铜	直径×印章高度	42.24×17.54
256	411	XC11632	YZ5650	铜	直径×印章高度	52.80×22.46
257	412	XC11641	YZ5659	铜	直径×印章高度	43.15×12.88
257	413	XC11607	YZ5625	铜	直径×印章高度	56.04×15.65
259	414	XC11863	YZ5881	铜	长×宽×印章高度	20.00×20.00×135.00
260	415	XC11864	YZ5882	银	长×宽×印章高度	16.00×15.00×160.00
261	416	XC11865	YZ5883	铜	直径×印章高度	15.00×64.00

道本同揆

止止山房捐赠西泠印社
域外印章集

All Truths Are One
Foreign Seals of Zhizhi Shanfang
Donated to Xiling Seal Engraver's Society

西泠印社 编
Edited by Xiling Seal Engraver's Society

何连海 主编
Chief Editor He Lianhai

印度河谷文明卷
Indus Valley Civilization Volume

别外卷
Extra Content Volume

西泠印社 出版社

图书在版编目（CIP）数据

道本同揆：止止山房捐赠西泠印社域外印章集 / 西泠印社编；何连海主编. -- 杭州：西泠印社出版社, 2025. 2. -- ISBN 978-7-5508-4775-0

Ⅰ. G262.1

中国国家版本馆CIP数据核字第2025PX2376号

道本同揆

止止山房捐赠西泠印社域外印章集

西泠印社 编　　何连海 主编

责任编辑	傅笛扬　张靓松
责任校对	曹　卓
责任印制	杨飞凤
装帧设计	杨　宇
出版发行	西泠印社出版社有限公司

（杭州市西湖文化广场32号5楼　邮政编码　310014）

经　　销	全国新华书店
制　　版	南京莱斯展览服务有限公司
印　　刷	南京新世纪联盟印务有限公司
开　　本	889mm×1194mm　1/16
字　　数	170千字
印　　张	33.25
书　　号	ISBN 978-7-5508-4775-0
版　　次	2025年2月第1版　第1次印刷
定　　价	580.00元（全二册）

版权所有　翻印必究　印制差错　负责调换

西泠印社出版社发行部联系方式：（0571）87243079

目　录

Contents

001—161	印度河谷文明卷 Indus Valley Civilization Volume
163—167	索引表 Index
169—240	别外卷 Extra Content Volume
241—243	索引表 Index
244	后记

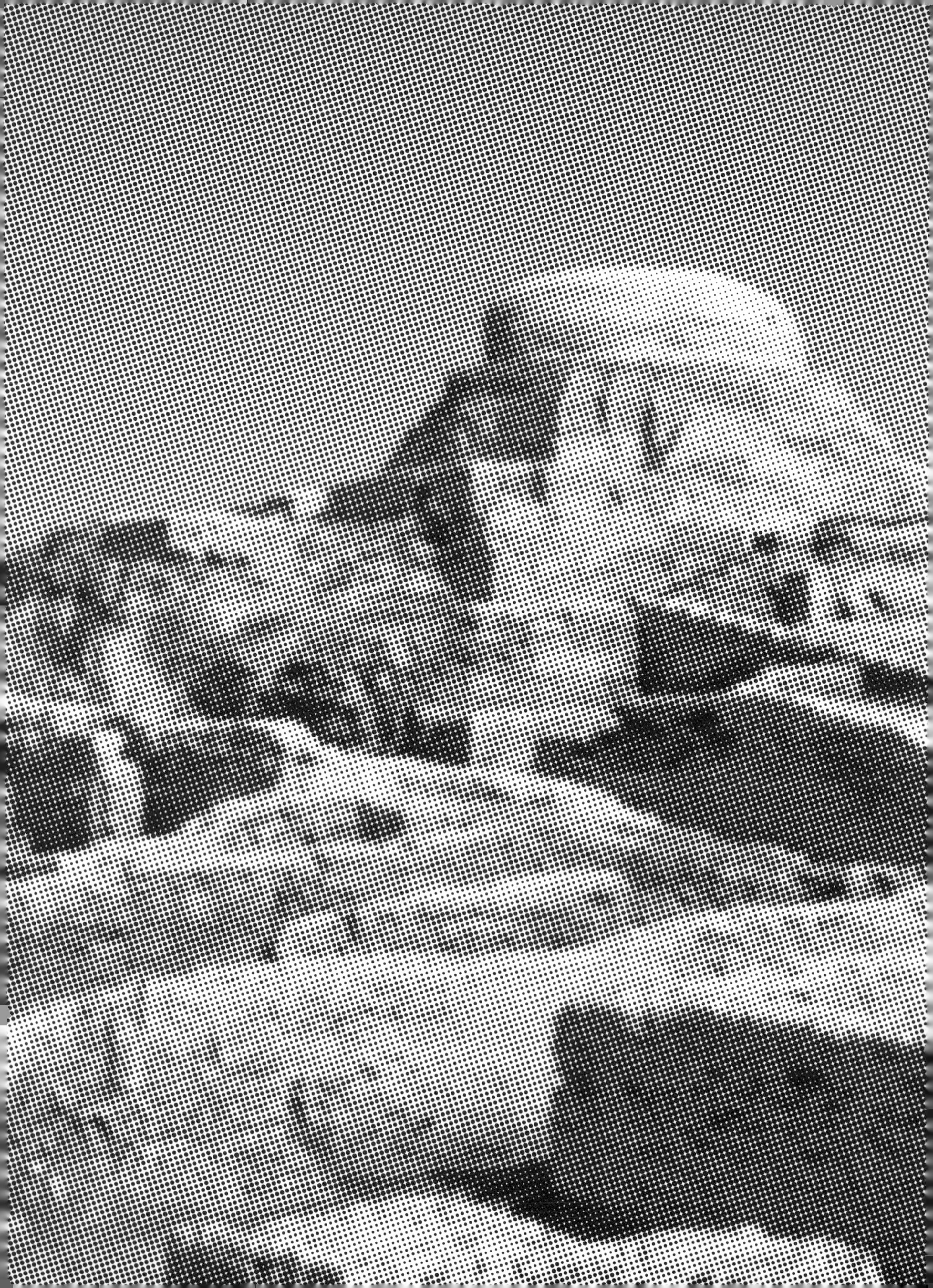

印度河谷文明卷
Indus Valley Civilization Volume

印度河谷文明

印度河谷文明（Indus Valley Civilization）是目前已知的南亚地区最发达的青铜时代文明，也是与古代埃及文明、古代两河文明、华夏文明并称为"四大文明"的人类早期文明之一。印度河谷文明起源于距今9000多年前的俾路支和信德平原的聚落文化，伴随着早期的石质及青铜质平印的出现，在公元前3600年前后发展到铜石并用时代。

公元前2500年至前1900年间，印度河谷及古吉拉特沿海一带成为新的文明中心，信德平原在印度河的冲击下有着肥沃的土地，这里盛产水稻和棉花，周边有着丰富的各类矿产资源。这里的先民先后兴建了哈拉帕（Harappa）、摩亨佐-达罗（Mohenjo-Daro）、昌胡-达罗（Chanhu-Daro）等一系列规模宏大、功能完善、布局严整的城市，该时期也被称为成熟哈拉帕时期（Mature Harappan Period）。他们使用统一的象形文字书写体系，有着完善而细致的度量衡系统和当时极为发达的首饰加工业和造船业。印度河谷人的直接贸易主要依靠海运，当地的商船自南亚次大陆西北部的港口城市洛塔尔（Lothal）起航，沿近海绕过阿拉伯半岛，经波斯湾南部的巴林群岛补给，最终抵达幼发拉底河和底格里斯河的入海口附近，与当地的苏美尔文明、阿卡德帝国交流。在两河文明的楔形文字材料记载中，印度河谷也被称为"抹露哈"（Meluhha）。

在这个成熟的贸易体系中，印章是必不可少的身份证明和契约工具。同时期的两河文明多使用滚筒印章，而印度河谷文明更青睐平印。印度河谷文明最典型的平印印身多呈正方形，是有一定厚度的块状，通常形制规整、棱角分明。印章的底面凹雕图文，背后在中央大多有凸起的半球形钮，印钮中间常有一道深槽，两侧有V形钻孔。这种印章多以当地盛产的块滑石（Steatite）雕刻制成，这种石材质地细腻，天然状态下非常柔软，莫氏硬度1—2，易于雕刻。印章在雕刻完成后，可用窑炉缓慢焙烧，使其表层失水硬结，形成一层坚硬光滑的烧结壳，莫氏硬度可达4，能够满足随身佩戴、频繁使用而不至于被快速磨损消耗的需求，因此也被称为"烧结滑石"。印度河谷的平印上常带有复杂程度不一的图案及文字，多为凹雕的立体图案，钤盖后的封泥上多呈现出细节突出的浅浮雕效果。印章的题材多为动物，常见题材为搭配祭坛的婆罗门牛或吉尔牛，另有人物、大象、犀牛、人饲虎等稀有题材。图案空白部分通常有铭文，为印度河谷特有的象形文字书写系统，至今仍未能破译。印度河谷文明时期也制作滚筒印章及其他特殊形制的印章，通常有孔，兼具印章和人体装饰品的属性，一些带有几何纹和高度抽象符号的印章可能是当时人们的护身符。

在两河文明的代表性城市如乌尔、基什等地的遗址中均曾有印度河谷文明的印章出土。波斯湾沿岸的青铜时代遗址中，也发现了类似印章的变化品种，这使得印度河谷文明的印章足以称为距今4000多年前，人类第一次全球化的标志物之一。

公元前2000年左右，可能因一系列灾难性事件的发生，如季风停滞导致印度河改道等，印度河谷的各个城市在短期内突然被废弃。曾盛极一时的古老文明逐渐衰落，四散奔逃的幸存者无力再制作这种精美复杂的印章，他们的文字传承也在公元前1700年左右断绝，直至公元19世纪以来的多次系统性考古发掘才得以重见天日。

综合现有考古证据和相关资料可以认为，印度河谷文明的印章在当时使用等级较高，整体存世量稀少，印章产地及年代明确固定，文化寓意明确。其产生和演化可能对后来世界范围内印章的应用和传承产生了极为重要的作用。

Indus Valley Civilization

The Indus Valley Civilization is currently known as the most developed Bronze Age civilization in Southern Asia and is one of the "Four Great Civilizations" of the first generation, alongside Ancient Egypt, Ancient Mesopotamia, and Chinese Civilization. It originated from the tribe culture of Baluchistan and the Sindh Plain more than 9000 years ago and evolved into the Chalcolithic Age around 3600 BC, with the emergence of early stone and bronze seals.

Between 2500 BCE and 1900 BCE, the Indus Valley and the coastal region of Gujarat became new centers of civilization. The Sindh Plain which was rich in mineral resources was fertile due to the alluvium from the Indus River, and abundant in rice and cotton. The ancestors here successively built a series of cities on a grand scale, which had complete functions and rigorous layout, such as Harappa, Mohenjo-Daro, and Chanhu-Daro. This period is also called as the Mature Harappan Period. They used a unified hieroglyphic writing system, having a sophisticated system of measurement and highly developed jewelry processing industry and shipbuilding industry at that time. Direct trade of the Indus Valley people mainly relied on sea transport. Local merchantmen sailed from the port city of Lothal in the northwest of the Indian subcontinent, bypassing the Arabian Peninsula along the coast while staying close to land, replenishing at the Bahrain Islands in the southern Persian Gulf, and finally arrived near the confluence of the Euphrates and Tigris Rivers to interact with the local Sumerian Civilization and Akkadian Empire. In the cuneiform records of Mesopotamian Civilization, the Indus Valley was also referred to as "Meluhha".

In this mature trade system, seals were indispensable for proof of identity and agreeing a contract. While Mesopotamian Civilization of the same period predominantly used cylinder seals, the Indus Valley Civilization favored flat seals. The typical seals of the Indus Valley Civilization were square and block-shaped with a certain thickness, usually well-designed and angular. The bottom of seal was engraved with intaglio patterns and inscription, and the top often had a convex hemispherical holder in the center, which has a deep groove in the middle and V-shaped drilling holes on both side. These seals were mostly engraved by the locally abundant steatite. The stone has a delicate texture and is naturally very soft, with a Mohs hardness of 1-2, making it easy to carve. After carving, the steatite could be slowly fired in a kiln to dehydrate and harden its surface, forming a hard and smooth sintered shell with Mohs hardness up to 4. This allowed the seal to be worn and frequently used without rapidly wearing away, making it known as "Fired Steatite". The seals of the Indus Valley often have patterns and inscription of varying complexity, mostly being intaglio and solid figures. After pressing into soft clay, the printing were in relief with prominent details. The subject matter was primarily animal. The common subject is Brahman bull or Gayal bull accompanied by altar, as well as rare subjects such as humankind, elephant, rhinoceros, and human rearing tiger. The blank parts of the patterns usually contained inscription in the unique hieroglyphic writing system of the Indus Valley, which has remained undeciphered until now. During the Indus Valley Civilization, cylinder seals and other specially shaped seals were also produced, usually with holes, serving both as seals and body ornaments. Some of these seals, featuring geometric patterns and highly abstract signs, may have been amulets worn by people at that time.

Seals of the Indus Valley Civilization have been unearthed at the ruins of representative Mesopotamian cities such as Ur and Kish, and variations of similar seals have been found at Bronze Age sites along the Persian Gulf coast. This makes the seals of the Indus Valley Civilization one of the hallmarks of first globalization in human history more than 4000 years ago.

Around 2000 BC, due to a series of catastrophic events, such as monsoon stagnation leading to the diversion of the Indus River, the cities of the Indus Valley were suddenly abandoned within a short period. An ancient civilization that once flourished gradually fell into decline, and the survivors who fled were unable to produce such exquisite and complex seals again. The written tradition of their language was also lost around 1700 BC and has been rediscovered through multiple systematic archaeological excavations since the 19th century.

Based on the existing archaeological evidence and related materials, it is believed that these seals were used at a high level at that time and the surviving are scarce in overall quantity. The origin and age of the Indus Valley Civilization seals are clearly fixed, with definite cultural meanings. Their emergence and evolution may have had an extremely important role in the application and inheritance of seals worldwide in later generations.

印度河谷文明　Indus Valley Civilization

001

题材
Subject Matter

动物（饲虎）+ 铭文
Animal (Rearing Tiger) & Inscription

001

印度河谷文明	Indus Valley Civilization	002	题材 Subject Matter
			动物（虎）+ 铭文 Animal (Tiger) & Inscription

002

印度河谷文明　Indus Valley Civilization	003	题材 Subject Matter
		动物（牛）+ 铭文 Animal (Bull) & Inscription

003

印度河谷文明 Indus Valley Civilization

004

题材
Subject Matter

动物（牛）+ 铭文
Animal (Bull) & Inscription

004

印度河谷文明　Indus Valley Civilization	005	题材 Subject Matter
		动物（犀牛）+ 铭文 Animal (Rhinoceros) & Inscription

005

印度河谷文明 Indus Valley Civilization   006

| 题材
| Subject Matter
|
| 动物（大象）+ 铭文
| Animal (Elephant) & Inscription

006

印度河谷文明 Indus Valley Civilization	007	题材 Subject Matter
		动物（独角兽）+ 铭文 Animal (Unicorn) & Inscription

印度河谷文明 Indus Valley Civilization 008

| 题材
| Subject Matter
|
| 动物（独角兽）+ 铭文
| Animal (Unicorn) & Inscription

008

印度河谷文明 Indus Valley Civilization

009

题材
Subject Matter

动物（独角兽）+ 铭文
Animal (Unicorn) & Inscription

009

印度河谷文明　Indus Valley Civilization

010

| 题材
| Subject Matter
|
| 动物（独角兽）+ 铭文
| Animal (Unicorn) & Inscription

010

015

印度河谷文明	Indus Valley Civilization	011	题材 Subject Matter
			动物（独角兽）+ 铭文 Animal (Unicorn) & Inscription

印度河谷文明   Indus Valley Civilization

012

题材
Subject Matter

动物（独角兽）+ 铭文
Animal (Unicorn) & Inscription

012

印度河谷文明 Indus Valley Civilization	013	题材 Subject Matter
		动物（独角兽）+ 铭文 Animal (Unicorn) & Inscription

013

印度河谷文明 Indus Valley Civilization

014

| 题材
| Subject Matter
|
| 动物（独角兽）+ 铭文
| Animal (Unicorn) & Inscription

014

印度河谷文明 Indus Valley Civilization

题材
Subject Matter

动物（独角兽）+ 铭文
Animal (Unicorn) & Inscription

印度河谷文明　Indus Valley Civilization	016	题材　Subject Matter
		动物（独角兽）+ 铭文 Animal (Unicorn) & Inscription

016

| 印度河谷文明 Indus Valley Civilization | 017 | 题材
Subject Matter

动物（独角兽）+ 铭文
Animal (Unicorn) & Inscription |

017

印度河谷文明 Indus Valley Civilization

018

| 题材
Subject Matter

动物（独角兽）+ 铭文
Animal (Unicorn) & Inscription

018

印度河谷文明　Indus Valley Civilization	019	题材　Subject Matter
		动物（独角兽）+ 铭文　Animal (Unicorn) & Inscription

019

印度河谷文明　Indus Valley Civilization

020

| 题材
| Subject Matter
|
| 动物（独角兽）+ 铭文
| Animal (Unicorn) & Inscription

020

| 印度河谷文明　Indus Valley Civilization | 021 | 题材
Subject Matter

动物（独角兽）+ 铭文
Animal (Unicorn) & Inscription |

021

印度河谷文明 Indus Valley Civilization

022

题材
Subject Matter

动物（独角兽）+ 铭文
Animal (Unicorn) & Inscription

022

| 印度河谷文明 Indus Valley Civilization | 023 | 题材
Subject Matter

动物（独角兽）+ 铭文
Animal (Unicorn) & Inscription |

023

印度河谷文明 Indus Valley Civilization 024

| 题材
| Subject Matter
|
| 动物（独角兽）+ 铭文
| Animal (Unicorn) & Inscription

024

印度河谷文明 Indus Valley Civilization	025	题材 Subject Matter
		动物（独角兽）+ 铭文 Animal (Unicorn) & Inscription

025

| 印度河谷文明 Indus Valley Civilization | 026 | 题材
Subject Matter |
| | | 动物（独角兽）+ 铭文
Animal (Unicorn) & Inscription |

026

印度河谷文明　Indus Valley Civilization

027

题材
Subject Matter

动物（独角兽）+ 铭文
Animal (Unicorn) & Inscription

027

印度河谷文明 Indus Valley Civilization

028

题材
Subject Matter

动物（独角兽）+ 铭文
Animal (Unicorn) & Inscription

028

印度河谷文明 Indus Valley Civilization

029

| 题材
| Subject Matter

动物（独角兽）+ 铭文
Animal (Unicorn) & Inscription

029

印度河谷文明　Indus Valley Civilization

030

| 题材
Subject Matter

动物（独角兽）+ 铭文
Animal (Unicorn) & Inscription

印度河谷文明　Indus Valley Civilization	031	题材 Subject Matter
		动物（独角兽）+ 铭文 Animal (Unicorn) & Inscription

031

印度河谷文明　Indus Valley Civilization

032

| 题材
Subject Matter

动物（独角兽）+ 铭文
Animal (Unicorn) & Inscription

032

| **印度河谷文明** Indus Valley Civilization | 033 | 题材
Subject Matter

动物（独角兽）+ 铭文
Animal (Unicorn) & Inscription |

印度河谷文明　Indus Valley Civilization

题材
Subject Matter

动物（独角兽）+ 铭文
Animal (Unicorn) & Inscription

| 印度河谷文明 Indus Valley Civilization | 035 | 题材
Subject Matter

动物（独角兽）+ 铭文
Animal (Unicorn) & Inscription |

035

印度河谷文明　Indus Valley Civilization

题材
Subject Matter
动物（独角兽）+ 铭文
Animal (Unicorn) & Inscription

| 印度河谷文明 Indus Valley Civilization | 037 | 题材 Subject Matter |
| | | 动物（独角兽）+ 铭文 Animal (Unicorn) & Inscription |

印度河谷文明　Indus Valley Civilization　038

| 题材
| Subject Matter
|
| 动物（独角兽）+ 铭文
| Animal (Unicorn) & Inscription

038

| 印度河谷文明 Indus Valley Civilization | 039 | 题材
Subject Matter

动物（独角兽）+ 铭文
Animal (Unicorn) & Inscription |

印度河谷文明 Indus Valley Civilization　　040

| 题材
Subject Matter

动物（独角兽）+ 铭文
Animal (Unicorn) & Inscription

040

印度河谷文明　Indus Valley Civilization

041

题材
Subject Matter

动物（独角兽）+ 铭文
Animal (Unicorn) & Inscription

041

印度河谷文明　Indus Valley Civilization

042

| 题材
| Subject Matter
|
| 动物（独角兽）+ 铭文
| Animal (Unicorn) & Inscription

042

| 印度河谷文明　Indus Valley Civilization | 043 | 题材
Subject Matter

动物（独角兽）+ 铭文
Animal (Unicorn) & Inscription |

印度河谷文明 Indus Valley Civilization   044

| 题材
| Subject Matter
|
| 动物（独角兽）+ 铭文
| Animal (Unicorn) & Inscription

044

印度河谷文明 Indus Valley Civilization	045	题材 Subject Matter
		动物（独角兽）+ 铭文 Animal (Unicorn) & Inscription

045

印度河谷文明　Indus Valley Civilization　046

| 题材
| Subject Matter
|
| 动物（独角兽）+ 铭文
| Animal (Unicorn) & Inscription

046

| 印度河谷文明 | Indus Valley Civilization |

047

| 题材
| Subject Matter

| 动物（独角兽）+ 铭文
| Animal (Unicorn) & Inscription

047

印度河谷文明 Indus Valley Civilization

048

题材
Subject Matter

动物（独角兽）+ 铭文
Animal (Unicorn) & Inscription

048

印度河谷文明　Indus Valley Civilization	049	题材 Subject Matter
		动物（独角兽）+ 铭文 Animal (Unicorn) & Inscription

049

印度河谷文明　Indus Valley Civilization

050

| 题材
| Subject Matter
|
| 动物（独角兽）+ 铭文
| Animal (Unicorn) & Inscription

050

| 印度河谷文明 Indus Valley Civilization | 051 | 题材
Subject Matter

动物（独角兽）+ 铭文
Animal (Unicorn) & Inscription |

051

印度河谷文明　Indus Valley Civilization　052

| 题材
| Subject Matter
|
| 动物（独角兽）+ 铭文
| Animal (Unicorn) & Inscription

052

印度河谷文明 Indus Valley Civilization		题材 Subject Matter
		动物（独角兽）+ 铭文 Animal (Unicorn) & Inscription

印度河谷文明 Indus Valley Civilization

054

题材
Subject Matter

动物（独角兽）+ 铭文
Animal (Unicorn) & Inscription

054

印度河谷文明	Indus Valley Civilization	055	题材 Subject Matter

动物（独角兽）+ 铭文
Animal (Unicorn) & Inscription

印度河谷文明　Indus Valley Civilization　　056

| 题材
| Subject Matter
|
| 动物（独角兽）+ 铭文
| Animal (Unicorn) & Inscription

056

印度河谷文明　Indus Valley Civilization　057

| 题材
Subject Matter

动物（独角兽）+ 铭文
Animal (Unicorn) & Inscription

057

印度河谷文明　Indus Valley Civilization　　058

题材 Subject Matter
动物（独角兽）+ 铭文 Animal (Unicorn) & Inscription

058

印度河谷文明 Indus Valley Civilization	059	题材 Subject Matter
		动物（独角兽）+ 铭文 Animal (Unicorn) & Inscription

059

印度河谷文明　Indus Valley Civilization　060

| 题材
| Subject Matter
|
| 动物（独角兽）+ 铭文
| Animal (Unicorn) & Inscription

060

印度河谷文明 Indus Valley Civilization	061	题材 Subject Matter
		动物（独角兽）+ 铭文 Animal (Unicorn) & Inscription

印度河谷文明 Indus Valley Civilization	062	题材 Subject Matter
		动物（独角兽）+ 铭文 Animal (Unicorn) & Inscription

062

| 印度河谷文明　Indus Valley Civilization | 063 | 题材
Subject Matter

动物（独角兽）+ 铭文
Animal (Unicorn) & Inscription |

印度河谷文明 Indus Valley Civilization

064

题材
Subject Matter

动物（独角兽）+ 铭文
Animal (Unicorn) & Inscription

064

印度河谷文明	Indus Valley Civilization	065	题材 Subject Matter

动物（独角兽）+ 铭文
Animal (Unicorn) & Inscription

印度河谷文明 Indus Valley Civilization   066

| 题材
| Subject Matter
|
| 动物（独角兽）+ 铭文
| Animal (Unicorn) & Inscription

066

印度河谷文明　Indus Valley Civilization	067	题材 Subject Matter
		动物（独角兽）+ 铭文 Animal (Unicorn) & Inscription

067

印度河谷文明　Indus Valley Civilization

068

| 题材
| Subject Matter
|
| 动物（独角兽）+ 铭文
| Animal (Unicorn) & Inscription

068

印度河谷文明　Indus Valley Civilization

069

| 题材
Subject Matter

动物（独角兽）+ 铭文
Animal (Unicorn) & Inscription

印度河谷文明 Indus Valley Civilization

070

| 题材
| Subject Matter
|
| 动物（独角兽）+ 铭文
| Animal (Unicorn) & Inscription

070

印度河谷文明	Indus Valley Civilization	071	题材 Subject Matter
			动物（独角兽）+ 铭文 Animal (Unicorn) & Inscription

071

印度河谷文明 Indus Valley Civilization   072

| 题材 |
| Subject Matter |
| 铭文 |
| Inscription |

072

印度河谷文明	Indus Valley Civilization	073	题材 Subject Matter
			铭文 Inscription

073

印度河谷文明 Indus Valley Civilization 074

| 题材 Subject Matter |
| 铭文 Inscription |

074

印度河谷文明 Indus Valley Civilization   075

| 题材 Subject Matter
| 铭文 Inscription

075

印度河谷文明　Indus Valley Civilization

076

| 题材 Subject Matter |
| 铭文 Inscription |

076

印度河谷文明 Indus Valley Civilization	077	题材 Subject Matter
		铭文（卐） Inscription（卐）

077

印度河谷文明 Indus Valley Civilization

题材
Subject Matter

铭文（卐）
Inscription（卐）

印度河谷文明　Indus Valley Civilization

0̇7̇9̇

| 题材
Subject Matter

| 铭文（卐）
Inscription（卐）

0̇7̇9̇

印度河谷文明 Indus Valley Civilization 080

| 题材 Subject Matter |
| 铭文 Inscription |

080

印度河谷文明　Indus Valley Civilization

081

| 题材
Subject Matter
| 铭文
Inscription

081

印度河谷文明 Indus Valley Civilization　082　| 题材
Subject Matter

| 铭文
Inscription

082

印度河谷文明	Indus Valley Civilization	083	题材 Subject Matter
			铭文 Inscription

083

印度河谷文明　Indus Valley Civilization　084

题材 Subject Matter
铭文 Inscription

084

| 印度河谷文明 Indus Valley Civilization | 085 | 题材 Subject Matter |
| | | 动物（独角兽）+ 铭文 Animal (Unicorn) & Inscription |

085

印度河谷文明	Indus Valley Civilization	086	题材 Subject Matter
			动物（独角兽）+ 铭文 Animal (Unicorn) & Inscription

086

印度河谷文明 Indus Valley Civilization

087

| 题材
Subject Matter

动物（独角兽）+ 铭文
Animal (Unicorn) & Inscription

087

印度河谷文明 Indus Valley Civilization

题材
Subject Matter

动物（独角兽）+ 铭文
Animal (Unicorn) & Inscription

| 印度河谷文明 Indus Valley Civilization | 089 | 题材
Subject Matter

动物（独角兽）+ 铭文
Animal (Unicorn) & Inscription |

印度河谷文明　Indus Valley Civilization　090

| 题材
| Subject Matter
|
| 铭文 / 动物（独角兽）+ 铭文
| Inscription / Animal (Unicorn) & Inscription

| 印度河谷文明 Indus Valley Civilization | 091 | 题材 Subject Matter |
| | | 动物 / 动物 Animal / Animal |

印度河谷文明 Indus Valley Civilization

092

| 题材
| Subject Matter
|
| 动物（羊）
| Animal (Goat)

092

印度河谷文明　Indus Valley Civilization

093

| 题材
Subject Matter

动物（羊）+ 铭文
Animal (Goat) & Inscription

093

印度河谷文明 Indus Valley Civilization

094

题材 Subject Matter
动物（羊）+ 铭文 Animal (Goat) & Inscription

094

印度河谷文明	Indus Valley Civilization	095	题材　Subject Matter
			铭文 / 动物（羊） Inscription / Animal (Goat)

印度河谷文明　Indus Valley Civilization　096

| 题材
| Subject Matter
|
| 铭文 / 动物（羊）
| Inscription / Animal (Goat)

096

印度河谷文明 Indus Valley Civilization

097

| 题材
| Subject Matter
|
| 铭文 / 动物（羊）
| Inscription / Animal (Goat)

097

印度河谷文明 Indus Valley Civilization

题材 Subject Matter
铭文 / 几何纹 Inscription / Geometry Pattern

| 印度河谷文明 Indus Valley Civilization | 099 | 题材 Subject Matter |
| | | 动物（鸟） Animal (Bird) |

099

印度河谷文明 Indus Valley Civilization	100	题材 Subject Matter
		动物（鹰）/ 动物（骆驼） Animal (Eagle) / Animal (Camel)

| 印度河谷文明　Indus Valley Civilization | 101 | 题材
Subject Matter

动物（马）/ 动物（狗）
Animal (Horse) / Animal (Dog) |

101

印度河谷文明 Indus Valley Civilization

题材
Subject Matter
动物
Animal

印度河谷文明 Indus Valley Civilization

103

| 题材
| Subject Matter
|
| 几何纹 / 几何纹
| Geometry Pattern / Geometry Pattern

| 印度河谷文明 Indus Valley Civilization | 104 | 题材
Subject Matter

几何纹 / 几何纹
Geometry Pattern / Geometry Pattern |

104

印度河谷文明　Indus Valley Civilization

105

| 题材
Subject Matter

动物（牛）+ 铭文
Animal (Bull) & Inscription

105

印度河谷文明　Indus Valley Civilization

题材
Subject Matter

动物（鹰）
Animal (Eagle)

印度河谷文明 Indus Valley Civilization	107	题材 Subject Matter
		动物 / 动物 / 几何纹 Animal / Animal / Geometry Pattern

印度河谷文明　Indus Valley Civilization

108

| 题材
| Subject Matter
|
| 几何纹
| Geometry Pattern

108

印度河谷文明 Indus Valley Civilization 109

题材
Subject Matter

几何纹
Geometry Pattern

109

印度河谷文明　Indus Valley Civilization　110

| 题材
| Subject Matter
|
| 植物 / 植物
| Plant / Plant

110

印度河谷文明 Indus Valley Civilization	111	题材 Subject Matter
		植物 / 植物 Plant / Plant

111

印度河谷文明　Indus Valley Civilization　112

| 题材
| Subject Matter
|
| 植物 / 植物
| Plant / Plant

112

| 印度河谷文明 Indus Valley Civilization | 113 | 题材
Subject Matter

几何纹 / 动物
Geometry Pattern / Animal |

113

印度河谷文明 Indus Valley Civilization

题材
Subject Matter

几何纹 / 几何纹
Geometry Pattern / Geometry Pattern

| 印度河谷文明　Indus Valley Civilization | 115 | 题材
Subject Matter

几何纹 / 几何纹
Geometry Pattern / Geometry Pattern |

115

印度河谷文明　Indus Valley Civilization

题材 Subject Matter
几何纹 Geometry Pattern

印度河谷文明 Indus Valley Civilization   117

题材 Subject Matter
几何纹 Geometry Pattern

117

| 印度河谷文明 Indus Valley Civilization | 118 | 题材
Subject Matter

几何纹
Geometry Pattern |

118

印度河谷文明 Indus Valley Civilization 119

| 题材 Subject Matter |
| 几何纹 Geometry Pattern |

119

印度河谷文明 Indus Valley Civilization

题材
Subject Matter

几何纹
Geometry Pattern

印度河谷文明 Indus Valley Civilization	121	题材 Subject Matter
		几何纹（阶梯纹） Geometry Pattern (Stair Pattern)

121

印度河谷文明　Indus Valley Civilization

122

| 题材
| Subject Matter
|
| 几何纹（阶梯纹）
| Geometry Pattern (Stair Pattern)

122

印度河谷文明　Indus Valley Civilization

1 2 3

题材
Subject Matter

几何纹
Geometry Pattern

1 2 3

印度河谷文明 Indus Valley Civilization

题材
Subject Matter

几何纹 / 植物
Geometry Pattern / Plant

130

印度河谷文明　Indus Valley Civilization　　125　| 题材
Subject Matter

| 隔珠印
Bead Seals for Interval

| 印度河谷文明 Indus Valley Civilization | 126 | 题材
Subject Matter

几何纹 / 动物（鸟）
Geometry Pattern / Animal (Bird) |

126

印度河谷文明　Indus Valley Civilization　127

| 题材
| Subject Matter
|
| 动物（双鱼）/ 植物
| Animal (A Couple of Fish) / Plant

127

印度河谷文明 Indus Valley Civilization 128

题材
Subject Matter

植物 / 动物（昆虫）
Plant / Animal (Insect)

印度河谷文明 Indus Valley Civilization

129

题材
Subject Matter

几何纹 / 几何纹
Geometry Pattern / Geometry Pattern

印度河谷文明 Indus Valley Civilization

130

| 题材
Subject Matter

几何纹 / 几何纹
Geometry Pattern / Geometry Pattern

130

印度河谷文明 Indus Valley Civilization

131

题材
Subject Matter

植物 / 植物
Plant / Plant

131

| 印度河谷文明 Indus Valley Civilization | 132 | 题材
Subject Matter

几何纹 / 植物
Geometry Pattern / Plant |

印度河谷文明　Indus Valley Civilization

| 题材
| Subject Matter
|
| 几何纹 / 植物
| Geometry Pattern / Plant

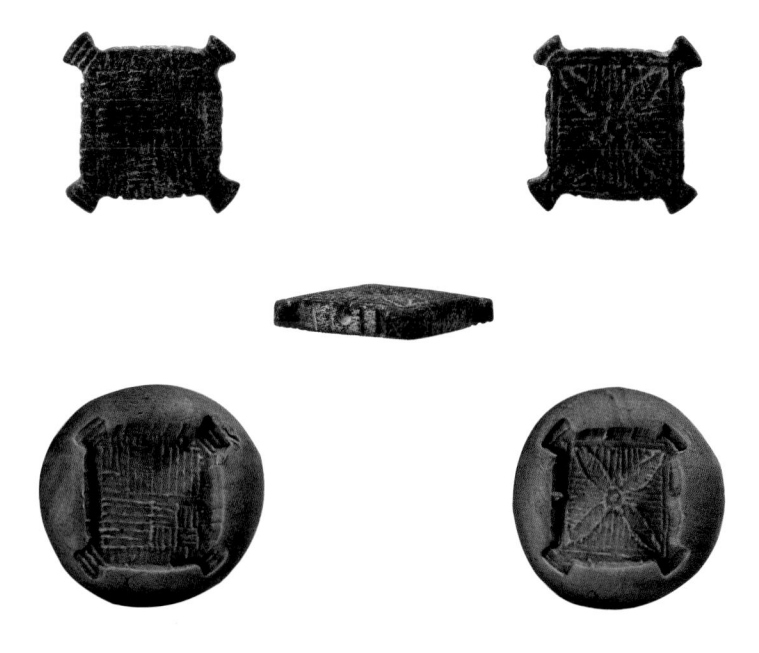

133

印度河谷文明	Indus Valley Civilization	134	题材 Subject Matter

几何纹 / 植物
Geometry Pattern / Plant

| 印度河谷文明 Indus Valley Civilization | 135 | 题材 Subject Matter |
| | | 几何纹 / 几何纹 Geometry Pattern / Geometry Pattern |

印度河谷文明 Indus Valley Civilization

136

题材
Subject Matter

几何纹 / 植物
Geometry Pattern / Plant

136

印度河谷文明 Indus Valley Civilization

137

题材
Subject Matter

几何纹 / 植物
Geometry Pattern / Plant

印度河谷文明　Indus Valley Civilization　　138

| 题材
| Subject Matter

| 几何纹 / 动物（昆虫）
| Geometry Pattern / Animal (Insect)

印度河谷文明 Indus Valley Civilization

139

题材
Subject Matter

动物（昆虫）/ 动物（昆虫）
Animal (Insect) / Animal (Insect)

印度河谷文明 Indus Valley Civilization	140	题材 Subject Matter
		植物 / 植物 Plant / Plant

140

146

印度河谷文明 Indus Valley Civilization

141

题材
Subject Matter

几何纹 / 植物
Geometry Pattern / Plant

141

印度河谷文明　Indus Valley Civilization

142

题材
Subject Matter

几何纹 / 植物
Geometry Pattern / Plant

印度河谷文明　Indus Valley Civilization

题材
Subject Matter

几何纹 / 几何纹
Geometry Pattern / Geometry Pattern

印度河谷文明 Indus Valley Civilization   144

| 题材
Subject Matter

| 几何纹 / 几何纹
Geometry Pattern / Geometry Pattern

印度河谷文明 Indus Valley Civilization

题材 Subject Matter
植物 / 动物 Plant / Animal

| 印度河谷文明 Indus Valley Civilization | 146 | 题材 Subject Matter |
| | | 几何纹 / 几何纹 Geometry Pattern / Geometry Pattern |

146

印度河谷文明　Indus Valley Civilization

147

| 题材
Subject Matter
| 几何纹
Geometry Pattern

147

| 印度河谷文明　Indus Valley Civilization | 148 | 题材
Subject Matter

几何纹 / 几何纹
Geometry Pattern / Geometry Pattern |

148

印度河谷文明 Indus Valley Civilization	题材 Subject Matter
	几何纹 / 几何纹 Geometry Pattern / Geometry Pattern

印度河谷文明	Indus Valley Civilization	150	题材 Subject Matter
			几何纹 / 几何纹 Geometry Pattern / Geometry Pattern

印度河谷文明 Indus Valley Civilization	151	题材 Subject Matter
		几何纹 / 几何纹 Geometry Pattern / Geometry Pattern

151

印度河谷文明	Indus Valley Civilization	152	题材 Subject Matter
			几何纹 Geometry Pattern

152

印度河谷文明 Indus Valley Civilization	153	题材 Subject Matter
		动物（鹰）/ 几何纹 Animal (Eagle) / Geometry Pattern

153

印度河谷文明 Indus Valley Civilization	154	题材 Subject Matter
		神话人物 / 动物 God / Animal

154

印度河谷文明 Indus Valley Civilization

155

题材
Subject Matter

动物 / 植物 + 动物（昆虫）
Animal / Plant & Animal (Insect)

155

印度河谷文明 Indus Valley Civilization

索引表
INDEX

页码	顺序	总账号	分类号	质料	测量方法	规格 (mm)
006	001	XC11807	YZ5825	烧结滑石	长 × 宽 × 印章高度	30.65×30.41×17.61
007	002	XC11854	YZ5872	烧结滑石	长 × 宽 × 印章高度	22.29×22.01×12.59
008	003	XC11806	YZ5824	烧结滑石	长 × 宽 × 印章高度	27.26×27.08×12.79
009	004	XC11737	YZ5755	烧结滑石	长 × 宽 × 印章高度	20.62×20.64×9.65
010	005	XC11824	YZ5842	烧结滑石	长 × 宽 × 印章高度	16.59×17.51×8.84
011	006	XC11810	YZ5828	烧结滑石	长 × 宽 × 印章高度	32.21×31.45×13.63
012	007	XC11845	YZ5863	烧结滑石	长 × 宽 × 印章高度	46.20×46.41×21.68
013	008	XC11759	YZ5777	烧结滑石	长 × 宽 × 印章高度	25.93×24.80×12.88
014	009	XC11819	YZ5837	烧结滑石	长 × 宽 × 印章高度	28.17×28.20×12.67
015	010	XC11820	YZ5838	烧结滑石	长 × 宽 × 印章高度	27.24×26.45×10.96
016	011	XC11818	YZ5836	烧结滑石	长 × 宽 × 印章高度	28.37×28.21×14.42
017	012	XC11817	YZ5835	烧结滑石	长 × 宽 × 印章高度	27.15×27.12×13.43
018	013	XC11811	YZ5829	烧结滑石	长 × 宽 × 印章高度	34.22×33.45×16.28
019	014	XC11822	YZ5840	烧结滑石	长 × 宽 × 印章高度	30.49×30.72×13.23
020	015	XC11809	YZ5827	烧结滑石	长 × 宽 × 印章高度	35.84×36.41×16.76
021	016	XC11808	YZ5826	烧结滑石	长 × 宽 × 印章高度	29.06×28.38×12.45
022	017	XC11805	YZ5823	烧结滑石	长 × 宽 × 印章高度	27.25×26.35×14.48
023	018	XC11804	YZ5822	烧结滑石	长 × 宽 × 印章高度	28.99×29.00×12.93
024	019	XC11803	YZ5821	烧结滑石	长 × 宽 × 印章高度	28.16×26.74×13.76
025	020	XC11815	YZ5833	烧结滑石	长 × 宽 × 印章高度	31.35×31.45×17.10
026	021	XC11814	YZ5832	烧结滑石	长 × 宽 × 印章高度	29.61×29.59×11.92
027	022	XC11816	YZ5834	烧结滑石	长 × 宽 × 印章高度	32.11×31.96×16.98
028	023	XC11812	YZ5830	烧结滑石	长 × 宽 × 印章高度	31.75×31.70×15.60
029	024	XC11802	YZ5820	烧结滑石	长 × 宽 × 印章高度	25.68×25.75×13.92
030	025	XC11821	YZ5839	烧结滑石	长 × 宽 × 印章高度	27.05×26.91×15.38

续表
CONTINUE THE TABLE

页码	顺序	总账号	分类号	质料	测量方法	规格 (mm)
031	026	XC11838	YZ5856	烧结滑石	长 × 宽 × 印章高度	25.20×24.79×13.56
032	027	XC11834	YZ5852	烧结滑石	长 × 宽 × 印章高度	22.37×23.19×12.58
033	028	XC11849	YZ5867	烧结滑石	长 × 宽 × 印章高度	25.31×24.21×11.92
034	029	XC11848	YZ5866	烧结滑石	长 × 宽 × 印章高度	26.53×26.41×16.49
035	030	XC11847	YZ5865	烧结滑石	长 × 宽 × 印章高度	26.83×26.63×13.77
036	031	XC11846	YZ5864	烧结滑石	长 × 宽 × 印章高度	26.19×26.05×11.15
037	032	XC11844	YZ5862	烧结滑石	长 × 宽 × 印章高度	26.55×26.25×11.92
038	033	XC11843	YZ5861	烧结滑石	长 × 宽 × 印章高度	26.32×25.88×11.53
039	034	XC11842	YZ5860	烧结滑石	长 × 宽 × 印章高度	26.63×25.86×10.48
040	035	XC11857	YZ5875	烧结滑石	长 × 宽 × 印章高度	26.93×25.96×11.60
041	036	XC11856	YZ5874	烧结滑石	长 × 宽 × 印章高度	26.65×26.67×13.62
042	037	XC11855	YZ5873	烧结滑石	长 × 宽 × 印章高度	25.37×25.51×13.39
043	038	XC11861	YZ5879	烧结滑石	长 × 宽 × 印章高度	26.04×26.32×11.84
044	039	XC11862	YZ5880	烧结滑石	长 × 宽 × 印章高度	26.68×26.67×13.77
045	040	XC11732	YZ5750	烧结滑石	长 × 宽 × 印章高度	20.01×19.72×11.06
046	041	XC11731	YZ5749	烧结滑石	长 × 宽 × 印章高度	19.91×19.89×10.44
047	042	XC11726	YZ5744	烧结滑石	长 × 宽 × 印章高度	18.33×17.98×9.53
048	043	XC11832	YZ5850	烧结滑石	长 × 宽 × 印章高度	13.85×14.70×8.04
049	044	XC11831	YZ5849	烧结滑石	长 × 宽 × 印章高度	17.28×17.33×9.79
050	045	XC11830	YZ5848	烧结滑石	长 × 宽 × 印章高度	16.58×16.54×10.16
051	046	XC11829	YZ5847	烧结滑石	长 × 宽 × 印章高度	18.26×17.88×10.71
052	047	XC11828	YZ5846	烧结滑石	长 × 宽 × 印章高度	17.78×17.63×8.20
053	048	XC11827	YZ5845	烧结滑石	长 × 宽 × 印章高度	14.85×15.05×9.29
054	049	XC11826	YZ5844	烧结滑石	长 × 宽 × 印章高度	16.86×16.14×9.70
055	050	XC11823	YZ5841	烧结滑石	长 × 宽 × 印章高度	18.29×18.11×11.71
056	051	XC11853	YZ5871	烧结滑石	长 × 宽 × 印章高度	20.67×19.29×13.71
057	052	XC11852	YZ5870	烧结滑石	长 × 宽 × 印章高度	21.26×20.99×13.64
058	053	XC11851	YZ5869	烧结滑石	长 × 宽 × 印章高度	19.99×20.51×8.44
059	054	XC11735	YZ5753	烧结滑石	长 × 宽 × 印章高度	20.24×20.57×10.93
060	055	XC11752	YZ5770	烧结滑石	长 × 宽 × 印章高度	23.70×23.22×9.75
061	056	XC11750	YZ5768	烧结滑石	长 × 宽 × 印章高度	22.58×23.02×12.48
062	057	XC11749	YZ5767	烧结滑石	长 × 宽 × 印章高度	22.97×22.88×10.15
063	058	XC11745	YZ5763	烧结滑石	长 × 宽 × 印章高度	22.32×21.48×10.83
064	059	XC11743	YZ5761	烧结滑石	长 × 宽 × 印章高度	24.11×23.79×13.13

续表
CONTINUE THE TABLE

页码	顺序	总账号	分类号	质料	测量方法	规格 (mm)
065	060	XC11837	YZ5855	烧结滑石	长 × 宽 × 印章高度	23.73×23.44×14.81
066	061	XC11836	YZ5854	烧结滑石	长 × 宽 × 印章高度	24.44×24.04×10.39
067	062	XC11835	YZ5853	烧结滑石	长 × 宽 × 印章高度	23.84×23.24×10.40
068	063	XC11841	YZ5859	烧结滑石	长 × 宽 × 印章高度	24.82×24.43×11.32
069	064	XC11840	YZ5858	烧结滑石	长 × 宽 × 印章高度	23.32×23.12×12.41
070	065	XC11839	YZ5857	烧结滑石	长 × 宽 × 印章高度	24.08×23.96×13.26
071	066	XC11860	YZ5878	烧结滑石	长 × 宽 × 印章高度	24.87×24.73×13.42
072	067	XC11858	YZ5876	烧结滑石	长 × 宽 × 印章高度	24.79×25.26×11.54
073	068	XC11813	YZ5831	烧结滑石	长 × 宽 × 印章高度	31.50×31.02×15.34
074	069	XC11859	YZ5877	滑石	长 × 宽 × 印章高度	25.87×25.02×13.04
075	070	XC11727	YZ5745	滑石	长 × 宽 × 印章高度	18.78×19.02×5.89
076	071	XC11850	YZ5868	滑石	长 × 宽 × 印章高度	21.73×21.53×8.41
077	072	XC11687	YZ5705	烧结滑石	长 × 宽 × 印章高度	13.28×12.99×6.62
078	073	XC11676	YZ5694	烧结滑石	长 × 宽 × 印章高度	11.18×11.30×4.68
079	074	XC11685	YZ5703	烧结滑石	长 × 宽 × 印章高度	12.50×12.88×8.17
080	075	XC11683	YZ5701	烧结滑石	长 × 宽 × 印章高度	12.48×12.01×7.15
081	076	XC11825	YZ5843	烧结滑石	长 × 宽 × 印章高度	14.42×14.33×8.06
082	077	XC11725	YZ5743	烧结滑石	长 × 宽 × 印章高度	18.02×17.41×9.42
083	078	XC11696	YZ5714	烧结滑石	长 × 宽 × 印章高度	14.43×14.43×8.03
084	079	XC11682	YZ5700	烧结滑石	长 × 宽 × 印章高度	12.34×12.39×7.30
085	080	XC11721	YZ5739	烧结滑石	长 × 宽 × 印章高度	17.17×17.68×5.27
086	081	XC11772	YZ5790	烧结滑石	长 × 宽 × 印章高度	24.83×14.88×29.07
087	082	XC11680	YZ5698	烧结滑石	长 × 宽 × 印章高度	12.11×12.27×5.16
088	083	XC11686	YZ5704	烧结滑石	长 × 宽 × 印章高度	12.62×13.16×6.58
089	084	XC11689	YZ5707	烧结滑石	长 × 宽 × 印章高度	13.44×13.35×7.17
090	085	XC11679	YZ5697	烧结滑石	长 × 宽 × 印章高度	12.05×12.26×6.98
091	086	XC11675	YZ5693	烧结滑石	长 × 宽 × 印章高度	11.27×11.03×5.15
092	087	XC11677	YZ5695	烧结滑石	长 × 宽 × 印章高度	11.57×11.45×6.65
093	088	XC11701	YZ5719	烧结滑石	长 × 宽 × 印章高度	14.54×15.37×7.69
094	089	XC11711	YZ5729	烧结滑石	长 × 宽 × 印章高度	16.76×16.76×8.28
095	090	XC11704	YZ5722	烧结滑石	长 × 宽 × 印章高度	15.43×9.17×4.23
096	091	XC11729	YZ5747	烧结滑石	长 × 宽 × 印章高度	19.49×13.77×7.36
097	092	XC11671	YZ5689	烧结滑石	长 × 宽 × 印章高度	9.60×9.56×6.09
098	093	XC11695	YZ5713	烧结滑石	长 × 宽 × 印章高度	14.28×13.91×8.37

续表
CONTINUE THE TABLE

页码	顺序	总账号	分类号	质料	测量方法	规格 (mm)
099	094	XC11833	YZ5851	烧结滑石	长×宽×印章高度	17.20×16.48×6.35
100	095	XC11691	YZ5709	烧结滑石	长×宽×印章高度	13.57×10.41×3.82
101	096	XC11708	YZ5726	烧结滑石	长×宽×印章高度	16.25×11.61×4.84
102	097	XC11688	YZ5706	烧结滑石	长×宽×印章高度	13.35×9.95×2.87
103	098	XC11712	YZ5730	烧结滑石	长×宽×印章高度	16.93×9.46×4.55
104	099	XC11709	YZ5727	烧结滑石	长×宽×印章高度	13.79×13.01×16.27
105	100	XC11765	YZ5783	大理石	直径×印章高度	22.62×10.57
106	101	XC11756	YZ5774	海螺	长×宽×印章高度	24.41×18.75×4.94
107	102	XC11718	YZ5736	费昂斯	长×宽×印章高度	17.49×17.05×11.04
108	103	XC11703	YZ5721	烧结滑石	底×高×印章高度	14.96×15.41×4.71
109	104	XC11771	YZ5789	骨质	直径×印章高度	20.03×31.13
109	104	XC11771	YZ5789	骨质	长轴×短轴×印章高度	20.36×14.60×31.13
110	105	XC11763	YZ5781	烧结滑石	直径×印章高度	32.63×28.00
111	106	XC11751	YZ5769	烧结滑石	底×高×印章高度	23.19×20.91×5.43
112	107	XC11742	YZ5760	烧结滑石	长×宽×印章高度	19.80×21.96×9.52
113	108	XC11684	YZ5702	烧结滑石	长×宽×印章高度	12.73×12.39×4.56
114	109	XC11699	YZ5717	烧结滑石	长×宽×印章高度	14.05×15.10×5.25
115	110	XC11674	YZ5692	烧结滑石	长×宽×印章高度	10.99×9.50×5.36
116	111	XC11692	YZ5710	烧结滑石	长×宽×印章高度	13.83×13.16×5.24
117	112	XC11673	YZ5691	烧结滑石	长×宽×印章高度	10.31×10.44×6.41
118	113	XC11717	YZ5735	烧结滑石	长×宽×印章高度	17.49×15.77×6.41
119	114	XC11670	YZ5688	烧结滑石	长×宽×印章高度	9.50×9.36×4.45
120	115	XC11739	YZ5757	烧结滑石	长×宽×印章高度	21.28×20.03×7.94
121	116	XC11690	YZ5708	烧结滑石	长×宽×印章高度	13.44×13.10×4.19
122	117	XC11672	YZ5690	海螺	长×宽×印章高度	9.66×9.29×6.77
123	118	XC11707	YZ5725	海螺	直径×印章高度	16.21×7.85
124	119	XC11744	YZ5762	烧结滑石	长×宽×印章高度	28.06×25.54×15.31
125	120	XC11730	YZ5748	烧结滑石	长×宽×印章高度	23.52×23.96×4.79
126	121	XC11764	YZ5782	烧结滑石	长×宽×印章高度	20.54×21.59×4.79
127	122	XC11706	YZ5724	烧结滑石	长×宽×印章高度	15.97×15.09×3.12
128	123	XC11710	YZ5728	烧结滑石	长×宽×印章高度	16.60×7.86×12.58
129	124	XC11702	YZ5720	滑石	长×宽×印章高度	17.29×22.73×6.36
131	125	XC11766	YZ5784	烧结滑石		
132	126	XC11736	YZ5754	滑石	长×宽×印章高度	16.82×17.45×5.46

续表
CONTINUE THE TABLE

页码	顺序	总账号	分类号	质料	测量方法	规格 (mm)
133	127	XC11705	YZ5723	滑石	长 × 宽 × 印章高度	19.67×19.01×17.45
134	128	XC11697	YZ5715	滑石	上底 × 下底 × 高 × 印章高度	11.43×26.05×18.20×4.90
135	129	XC11740	YZ5758	滑石	上底 × 下底 × 高 × 印章高度	14.92×25.02×17.60×5.16
136	130	XC11719	YZ5737	滑石	上底 × 下底 × 高 × 印章高度	14.57×26.75×17.78×5.23
137	131	XC11698	YZ5716	滑石	长 × 宽 × 印章高度	28.65×27.99×6.40
138	132	XC11715	YZ5733	滑石	长 × 宽 × 印章高度	23.06×23.25×5.30
139	133	XC11714	YZ5732	滑石	长 × 宽 × 印章高度	24.21×24.21×4.99
140	134	XC11733	YZ5751	滑石	长 × 宽 × 印章高度	27.66×27.95×5.88
141	135	XC11720	YZ5738	滑石	长 × 宽 × 印章高度	25.23×24.05×6.75
142	136	XC11700	YZ5718	滑石	长 × 宽 × 印章高度	25.42×25.67×6.31
143	137	XC11728	YZ5746	滑石	直径 × 印章高度	28.22×7.61
144	138	XC11722	YZ5740	滑石	直径 × 印章高度	19.04×6.25
145	139	XC11741	YZ5759	滑石	直径 × 印章高度	17.88×6.09
146	140	XC11693	YZ5711	滑石	直径 × 印章高度	32.61×8.04
147	141	XC11724	YZ5742	滑石	直径 × 印章高度	33.37×6.75
148	142	XC11734	YZ5752	滑石	直径 × 印章高度	23.62×6.04
149	143	XC11681	YZ5699	烧结滑石	直径 × 印章高度	12.38×5.24
150	144	XC11678	YZ5696	烧结滑石	直径 × 印章高度	12.22×4.39
151	145	XC11716	YZ5734	烧结滑石	直径 × 印章高度	17.47×7.92
152	146	XC11723	YZ5741	烧结滑石	直径 × 印章高度	17.80×6.29
153	147	XC11694	YZ5712	烧结滑石	直径 × 印章高度	14.15×9.91
154	148	XC11713	YZ5731	铜	底 × 高 × 印章高度	16.95×15.61×6.25
155	149	XC11738	YZ5756	铜	十字线 1× 十字线 2× 印章高度	20.96×20.32×6.43
156	150	XC11757	YZ5775	铜	十字线 1× 十字线 2× 印章高度	26.18×26.09×8.88
157	151	XC11413	YZ5431	铜	十字线 1× 十字线 2× 印章高度	27.26×26.41×6.84
158	152	XC11773	YZ5791	滑石	底 × 高 × 印章高度	45.44×42.03×16.24
159	153	XC11770	YZ5788	滑石	十字线 1× 十字线 2× 印章高度	30.36×30.64×5.76
160	154	XC11776	YZ5794	绿泥石	直径 × 印章高度	43.64×9.55
161	155	XC11519	YZ5537	大理石	直径 × 印章高度	18.92×43.24

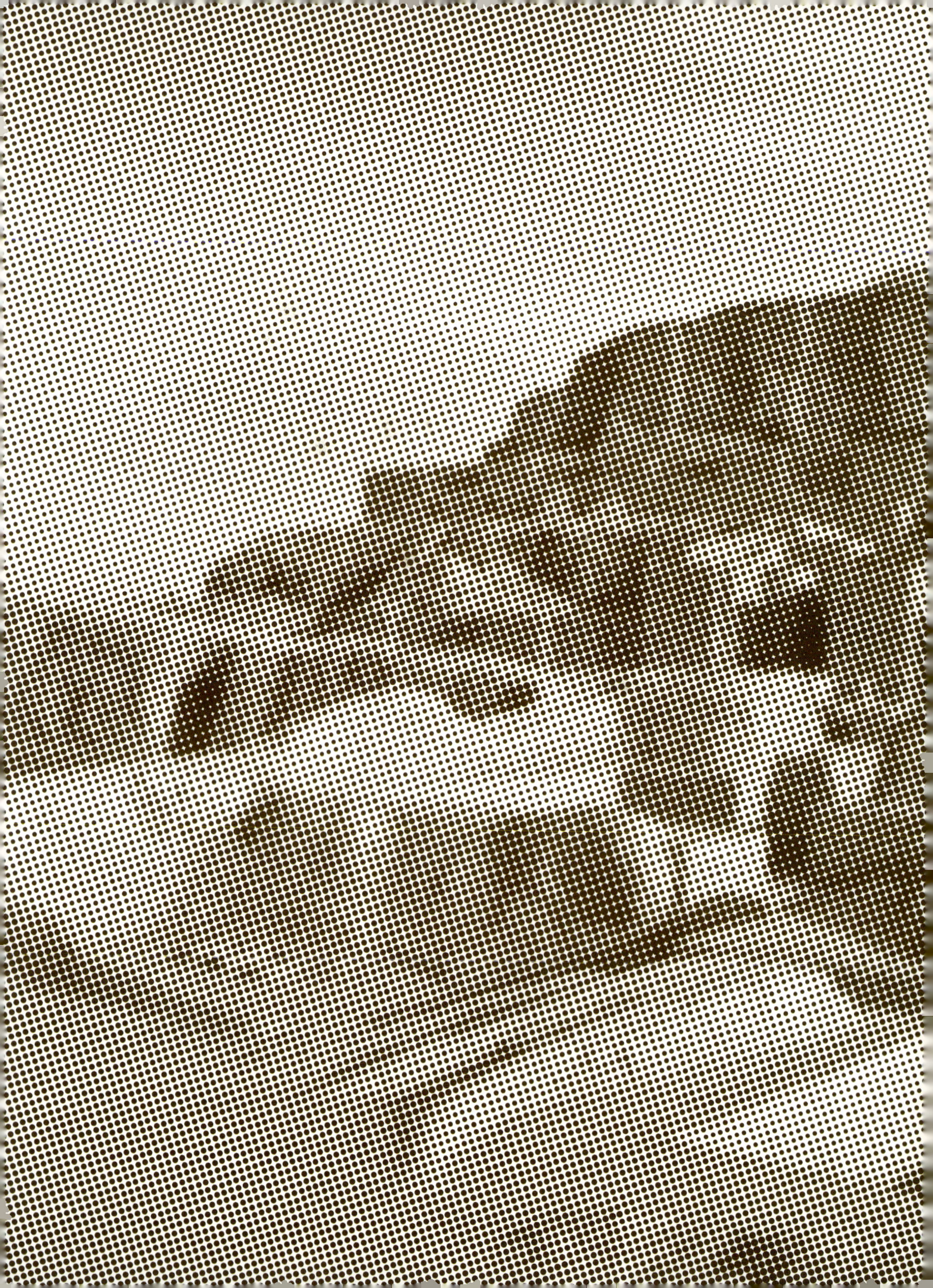

別外卷

Extra Content Volume

别外卷

印章是人类社会产生阶级性和人们形成自我身份认知的标志之一。作为社会生产关系复杂化的必然产物，印章的实际功能、形状材质、艺术风格、文化寓意具有地域差异，并随着时代的发展不断演化。

目前，印章最早出现在什么地方并无定论，但可以肯定的是，世界范围内不同文化的早期印章必然有着相对独立的起源。不同区域文化的印章虽然在发展历程中有借鉴和融合，但整体还是按照主体文化和时代发展出了不同的风格。从区域方面来说，古代印章大致可分为西亚、中亚与南亚、地中海沿岸、东亚和欧洲等。

目前已知最早的印章出自西亚两河流域北部的哈拉夫文化和小亚细亚的安纳托利亚文化，距今大约8000—7000年。这些印章大多是以当地常见的石材雕刻而成的平面印章，兼具功能性和装饰性，其出现的年代早于文字与文明的诞生。纹饰以简单的几何纹样或高度抽象化的人物、动物等为主，但有些印章同时会被雕刻成动物形状。这一传统在西亚一直流行至青铜时代，伊朗、叙利亚、伊拉克、土耳其等地的古老文化中均有类似设计理念的早期印章，可能为图形印的早期形态。但这类印章的属性和功能与阿克瑟斯文明的青铜印章一样未能定论，一方面被发现的使用证据难以确认其印章属性；另一方面当时印章的不同纹饰似乎很难实现识别个人身份的功能。

此后，真正意义上的印章随着楔形文字书写体系的成熟而出现。两河流域的先民用削成尖头的木棍或芦苇秆在湿润的黏土平面上书写文字，待晒干或烘干后即可形成泥板文书，由于这样书写出的文字笔画类似楔子，故名楔形文字。为证明关联者的身份，有些泥板文书表面会加盖印章。两河流域的乌鲁克人最早在圆筒形的珠子表面雕刻环绕的图案，这种印章钤盖在湿软的泥板上，可以形成一幅连贯的循环式的平面图案，因此也被称为滚筒印章（Cylinder Seal）。滚筒印章是两河文明最重要的印章形式，在其3000年的发展历程中，形成了不同时代和区域的风格，主要以精细的图案搭配印刻铭文为主，且非常注重纹饰的立体性表达。这种设计理念影响了印度河谷、阿克瑟斯、埃及及埃兰文明的印章体系，不过随着两河文明和楔形文字书写体系的消亡，滚筒印章的大规模制作与使用在波斯帝国阿契美尼德王朝时期断绝。波斯人建立的几个大型帝国在伊斯兰化之前一直有使用印章的传统，阿契美尼德王朝从两河文明吸收了滚印体系和起源于小亚细亚、盛行于新亚述及巴比伦时期的平印体系，其中金字塔形或圆锥形平印在此后依然盛行并占据主流，至萨珊王朝时期演化为半球形或半珠形平印，与希腊罗马式用于镶嵌的凹雕蛋面宝石共同使用。萨珊王朝时期全民用印，印章不仅作为普遍的身份象征，也广泛作为护身符和装饰品融入当时的流行风尚、宗教祭祀、行政事务等领域。

地中海沿岸的印章可包含埃及文明和主要受埃及影响黎凡特地区，以及北部爱琴海周边的爱琴文明。埃及文明的印章可能与早期两河文明有关，距今5000年前的埃及前王朝和早王朝时期出土了一些风格与同时期两河文明差别较大的滚筒印章，且在地中海上的塞浦路斯和黎凡特一带也依稀可见早期风格印章传播的证据。不过由于书写体系和书写介质不同，埃及的滚筒印章并不常见，当地更喜欢在金属、石材、费昂斯（釉砂）和玻璃等材质上制作平面印章，且非常注重印章形状的设计，其中最负盛名的当属古埃及的圣甲虫印珠。这类印珠盛行于古埃及中王国至王朝末期，背面雕刻圣甲虫（即蜣螂）形象，平坦的底面雕刻印纹，印纹多为由埃及铭文和一些抽象符号组成的平面纹饰。圣甲虫印章广为流传，在地中海沿岸的伊特鲁里亚、希腊、腓尼基等文明以及伊朗和阿拉伯半岛南部的诸多文明中均有同类印章出现。

在青铜时代，爱琴海的米诺斯人也开始制作印章，其印章风格较为独特。他们常在一些扁平设计的珠饰表面，以凹雕技法刻划纹饰，早期多见抽象的复杂几何纹，后期可见到风格写实生动的各类动物、神话场景，来源可能受到青铜时代两河文明的影响。这些印章同样很少雕刻铭文，难以确证其具体是否作为印章使用。不过它确实是后期希腊罗马印章及宝石雕刻艺术的重要源头。而希腊罗马时期的各类精雕细琢的宝石印章或蛋面珠宝则构成了铁器时代图形印章的最主要形态，深刻影响了近现代欧洲印鉴体系的形成。

除此之外，中亚青铜时代的阿克楚斯文明和南亚青铜时代的印度河谷文明都已在前两卷进行描述。铁器时代的中亚与南亚主要受到西亚、欧洲、阿拉伯等外来文明的先后影响，逐渐失去了其独有的文化特性。

在整个世界范围内，可能有独立起源、自身发展脉络清晰且从古至今从未断绝的印章体系唯有华夏文明的文字印系统。中国的印章系统经过了不同历史时期的对外交流和发展，可以作为一条连贯的时间轴与域外诸文明互相参照，为世界文明的发展脉络提供可靠而有序的印证。

Extra Content Volume

The appearance of seal is one of the hallmarks in the emergence of class structure in human society and the formation of people's recognition of self-identity. As an inevitable outcome of the increasing complexity of production relations, the practical functions, designs, materials, artistic styles, and cultural meanings of seals varied regionally and continuously evolved in response to the passage of time.

There remains no conclusion regarding the earliest origin of seals up to date. However, it is definite that the early seals of diverse cultures across the globe must have relatively independent origins. Despite the fact that seals from various regional cultures drew inspiration from and integrated with each another during their evolution, they nonetheless developed unique styles in accordance with their respective culture and historical periods broadly. From the perspective of the location of civilization, ancient seals can be generally categorized into those of Western Asia, Central and Southern Asia, Mediterranean region, Eastern Asia, Europe and so on.

The earliest known seals originated from the Halaf Culture in the northern areas of the Mesopotamia and the Anatolian Culture in Asia Minor, dating back to approximately 8000-7000 years ago. These seals were predominantly flat and engraved by locally available stones, combing functions of practical use and ornament. They emerged before writing and civilization, whose decorations primarily consisted of simple geometric patterns or highly abstract figure and animal patterns. Nonetheless some were also carved into animal shapes. This tradition endured in Western Asia until the Bronze Age, and similar design concepts existed in the early seals of ancient cultures in Iran, Syria, Iraq, Turkey, and other regions, possibly being the early forms of graphic seals. Nevertheless, the properties and functions of these seals, as well as those of the bronze seals of the Oxus Civilization, remain uncertain. On one hand, existing evidence of their use is challenging to demonstrate its use as seals. On the other hand, the distinctive decorative patterns of these seals appear hard to perform the function of identity verification.

Subsequently, definite seals emerged with the maturity of the cuneiform writing system. The ancients of Mesopotamia used sharpened wooden sticks or reeds to write on wet clay, which formed clay tablets after drying. The strokes of the written characters resembled cuneus, hence called as cuneiform. To authenticate the identity of the associated individuals, some clay tablets were stamped with seals. The Uruk people of Mesopotamia were the first to carve circular patterns on the surface of cylindrical beads. When pressed onto wet clay tablets, these seals could create a coherent, circular planar pattern, thus also known as cylinder seals. Cylinder seals were the most important form of seals in Mesopotamian Civilization. Over the course of 3000 years of development, they evolved into different styles in different periods and regions, featuring intricate patterns accompanied by inscription and emphasizing the solid expression of decorations. This design concept influenced the seal systems of the Indus Valley, Oxus, Egypt, and Elam civilizations. However, with the disappearance of Mesopotamian civilization and the cuneiform writing system, the mass production and use of cylinder seals ceased during the Achaemenid Dynasty of the Persian Empire. The several large empires established by the Persians maintained the tradition of using seals before their Islamization. The Achaemenid Dynasty adopted both the cylinder seal system from Mesopotamian civilization and the flat seal system which originated in Asia Minor and was prevalent during the Neo-Assyrian and Babylonian period. Among them, pyramid-shaped or conical flat seals remained popular and dominant thereafter, evolving into hemispherical or semi-bead-shaped seals during the Sassanian Dynasty, which were used alongside Greek-Roman style intaglio carved cabochons for inlaying. During the Sassanian Dynasty, seals were used by everyone, serving not only as a common symbol of identity but also widely as talismans and ornaments integrated into popular fashion, religious rituals, administrative affairs, and other fields.

The seals along the Mediterranean coast encompass Egyptian Civilization and the Levant region which is mainly influenced by Egypt, as well as the Aegean Civilization surrounding the northern Aegean Sea. The seals of Egyptian Civilization may be related to the early Mesopotamian Civilization. Some unearthed cylinder seals of the Predynastic and Early Dynastic periods of Egypt dating back to 5,000 years ago show styles quite different from those of contemporaneous Mesopotamian Civilization. There is also faint evidence of the spread of early-style seals in Mediterranean Cyprus and the Levant region. However, due to difference in writing system and writing media, cylinder seals are not common in Egypt, where seals made of metal, stone, faience, glass, and other materials are preferred and layed great emphasis on the design of seal shape. Among them, the most renowned are the scaraboid bead seals of ancient Egypt, which are prevalent from the Middle Kingdom to the Late Period. These bead seals are engraved scarabs (dung beetles) on the back and inscription on the flat bases, mostly consisting of Egyptian inscription and abstract signs of planar decorations. Scarab seals are widely circulated and the similar appear in civilizations along the Mediterranean coast, such as Etruria, Greece, Phoenicia, as well as many civilizations in Iran and the southern Arabian Peninsula.

During the Bronze Age, the Minoans of the Aegean Sea also began making seals with a unique style. They often carved decorations on the surface of flat-designed beads using intaglio techniques. Early examples featured abstract and complex geometric patterns, while later showed realistic and vivid depictions of various animals and mythical scenes, possibly influenced by the Mesopotamian Civilization of Bronze Age. These seals rarely carried inscription, making it difficult to confirm their specific use as seals. However, they were indeed important sources of later Greek and Roman seals and art of gemstone engraving. The intricately carved gemstone seals or jewelry cabochons over the Greek and Roman period constituted the main form of graphic seals in the Iron Age and profoundly influenced the birth of modern European seal system.

Besides, the Oxus Civilization of Central Asia and the Indus Valley Civilization of Southern Asia in Bronze Age have been depicted in previous volumes. During the Iron Age, Central Asia and Southern Asia were mainly influenced by external civilizations from Western Asia, Europe, and Arabia, gradually losing their unique cultural characteristics.

Globally, the seal system of Chinese Civilization having its possibly independent origin, clear development trajectory, and uninterrupted existence from ancient times to the present is the only one. Along with foreign exchanges and development in different historical periods, the Chinese seal system can serve as a coherent timeline for comparison with other civilizations, providing reliable and orderly evidence for the development of world civilizations.

别外卷 Extra Content Volume

001

题材 Subject Matter	地域 Region
几何纹 Geometry Pattern	西亚 Western Asia
质料 Material	时期 Period
绿泥石 Chlorite	欧贝德时期 Ubaid Period (6500-3800BC)

001

174

别外卷 Extra Content Volume　　002

题材 Subject Matter	地域 Region
几何纹 Geometry Pattern	西亚 Western Asia
质料 Material	时期 Period
绿泥石 Chlorite	欧贝德时期 Ubaid Period (6500-3800BC)

002

175

别外卷 Extra Content Volume   003

题材 Subject Matter	地域 Region
动物 Animal	西亚 Western Asia
质料 Material	时期 Period
绿泥石 Chlorite	欧贝德时期 Ubaid Period (6500-3800BC)

003

别外卷 Extra Content Volume

004

题材 Subject Matter	地域 Region
几何纹 Geometry Pattern	西亚 Western Asia
质料 Material	时期 Period
绿泥石 Chlorite	欧贝德时期 Ubaid Period (6500-3800BC)

004

177

别外卷 Extra Content Volume   005

题材 Subject Matter	地域 Region
动物 Animal	西亚 Western Asia
质料 Material	时期 Period
绿泥石 Chlorite	苏萨Ⅱ期 Susa II Period (4700-3400BC)

005

别外卷 Extra Content Volume 006

题材 Subject Matter	地域 Region
动物 Animal	西亚 Western Asia

质料 Material	时期 Period
大理石 Marble	苏萨Ⅱ期 Susa II Period (4700-3400BC)

006

别外卷 Extra Content Volume 007

题材 Subject Matter	地域 Region
几何纹 Geometry Pattern	西亚 Western Asia
质料 Material	时期 Period
陶 Clay	青铜时代晚期 Late Bronze Age (1500-1100BC)

007

別外卷 Extra Content Volume

181

别外卷 Extra Content Volume

008

题材 Subject Matter	地域 Region
几何纹 Geometry Pattern	西亚 Western Asia
质料 Material	时期 Period
绿泥石 Chlorite	青铜时代晚期 Late Bronze Age (1500-1100BC)

008

别外卷 Extra Content Volume 009

题材 Subject Matter	地域 Region
动物 + 几何纹 Animal & Geometry Pattern	西亚 Western Asia
质料 Material	时期 Period
绿泥石 Chlorite	赫梯帝国（穆尔西里二世） Hittite (Muwatallill) (1321-1295BC)

009

别外卷 Extra Content Volume

010

题材 Subject Matter	地域 Region
几何纹 Geometry Pattern	地中海东部 Eastern Mediterranean
质料 Material	时期 Period
绿泥石 Chlorite	铁器时代Ⅱ期 Iron Age Phase II (1000-700BC)

010

别外卷 Extra Content Volume   011

题材 Subject Matter	地域 Region
铭文 Inscription	古埃及 Ancient Egypt
质料 Material	时期 Period
费昂斯 Faience	埃及新王国时期 New Kingdom of Egypt (1553-1085BC)

011

别外卷 Extra Content Volume

012

题材 Subject Matter	地域 Region
铭文 Inscription	古埃及 Ancient Egypt
质料 Material	时期 Period
费昂斯 Faience	埃及新王国时期 New Kingdom of Egypt (1553-1085BC)

012

别外卷 Extra Content Volume	013	题材 Subject Matter	地域 Region
		人物 + 铭文 Humankind & Inscription	迦南，古埃及 Canaan, Ancient Egypt
		质料 Material	时期 Period
		费昂斯 Faience	埃及王朝后期 Late Period of Egypt (700-300BC)

013

别外卷 Extra Content Volume　　014

题材 Subject Matter	地域 Region
动物 Animal	地中海东部 Eastern Mediterranean
质料 Material	时期 Period
绿泥石 Chlorite	铁器时代 II 期 Iron Age Phase II (1000-700BC)

014

别外卷 Extra Content Volume   015

题材 Subject Matter	地域 Region
动物 Animal	叙利亚北部 Northern Syria
质料 Material	时期 Period
绿泥石 Chlorite	铁器时代Ⅱ期 Iron Age Phase II (1000-600BC)

015

别外卷 Extra Content Volume　　016

题材 Subject Matter	地域 Region
神话人物 God	两河流域 Mesopotamia
质料 Material	时期 Period
滑石 Steatite	新亚述帝国 Neo-Assyrian Empire (911-609BC)

016

别外卷 Extra Content Volume   017

题材 Subject Matter	地域 Region
动物 Animal	叙利亚北部 Northern Syria
质料 Material	时期 Period
绿泥石 Chlorite	铁器时代 II 期 Iron Age Phase II (1000-600BC)

017

别外卷 Extra Content Volume	018	题材 Subject Matter	地域 Region
		动物 Animal	小亚细亚 Asia Minor
		质料 Material	时期 Period
		绿泥石 Chlorite	青铜时代晚期 Late Bronze Age (1500-1100BC)

018

题材 Subject Matter	地域 Region
动物 Animal	中亚 Central Asia
质料 Material	时期 Period
滑石 Steatite	阿克瑟斯文明 Oxus Civilization (2200-1700BC)

别外卷 Extra Content Volume 020

题材 Subject Matter	地域 Region
人物 Humankind	中亚 Central Asia
质料 Material	时期 Period
铜 Copper	阿克瑟斯文明 Oxus Civilization (2300-1800BC)

别外卷 Extra Content Volume	021	题材 Subject Matter	地域 Region
		人物 + 动物 Humankind & Animal	中亚 Central Asia
		质料 Material	时期 Period
		铜 Copper	贵霜帝国 Kushan Empire (105-250AD)

别外卷 Extra Content Volume   022

题材 Subject Matter	地域 Region
几何纹 Geometry Pattern	伊朗东部或马尔吉亚纳 Eastern Iran or Margiana
质料 Material	时期 Period
铜合金 Copperalloy	阿克瑟斯文明早期 Early Oxus Civilization (2500-2000BC)

022

别外卷 Extra Content Volume	023	题材 Subject Matter	地域 Region
		几何纹 Geometry Pattern	中亚 Central Asia
		质料 Material	时期 Period
		铜 Copper	阿克瑟斯文明 Oxus Civilization (2300-1700BC)

023

别外卷 Extra Content Volume　　024

题材 Subject Matter	地域 Region
几何纹 Geometry Pattern	中亚 Central Asia
质料 Material	时期 Period
铜 Copper	阿克瑟斯文明 Oxus Civilization (2300-1700BC)

024

别外卷 Extra Content Volume	025	题材 Subject Matter	地域 Region
		几何纹 Geometry Pattern	中亚 Central Asia
		质料 Material	时期 Period
		铜 Copper	阿克瑟斯文明 Oxus Civilization (2300-1700BC)

025

别外卷 Extra Content Volume 026

题材 Subject Matter	地域 Region
动物 Animal	南亚 South Asia
质料 Material	时期 Period
铜 Copper	犍陀罗国 Gandhara (300-700AD)

026

别外卷 Extra Content Volume

027

题材 Subject Matter	地域 Region
动物 Animal	中亚 Central Asia
质料 Material	时期 Period
铜 Copper	铁器时代早期 Early Iron Age (1500-1000BC)

027

别外卷 Extra Content Volume	028	题材 Subject Matter	地域 Region
		几何纹 Geometry Pattern	中亚 Central Asia
		质料 Material	时期 Period
		铜 Copper	铁器时代早期 Early Iron Age (1500-1000BC)

028

别外卷 Extra Content Volume	029	题材 Subject Matter 几何纹 Geometry Pattern	地域 Region 伊朗西北部 Northwestern Iran
		质料 Material 铜 Copper	时期 Period 卢里斯坦文化 Luristan Culture (1200-700BC)

029

别外卷 Extra Content Volume   030

题材 Subject Matter	地域 Region
几何纹 Geometry Pattern	中亚 Central Asia

质料 Material	时期 Period
铜 Copper	铁器时代 Iron Age (500BC-500AD)

030

别外卷 Extra Content Volume	031	题材 Subject Matter	地域 Region
		动物 Animal	中亚 Central Asia
		质料 Material	时期 Period
		玛瑙	希腊巴克特里亚王国 Greco-Bactrian Kingdom (400-200BC)

031

别外卷 Extra Content Volume 032

题材 Subject Matter	地域 Region
动物（双羊纹） Animal (A Couple of Goat Pattern)	中亚 Central Asia
质料 Material	时期 Period
铜 Copper	200BC-200AD

032

别外卷 Extra Content Volume 033

题材 Subject Matter	地域 Region
动物（鱼化龙纹） Animal (Fish-dragon Transformation Pattern)	巴克特里亚或伊朗东部 Bactria or Eastern Iran

质料 Material	时期 Period
铜 Copper	1-200AD

033

别外卷 Extra Content Volume　　034

题材 Subject Matter	地域 Region
神话人物 God	南亚 South Asia

质料 Material	时期 Period
铜 Copper	贵霜帝国 Kushan Empire (100-300AD)

034

别外卷 Extra Content Volume	035	题材 Subject Matter	地域 Region
		几何纹 Geometry Pattern	南亚 South Asia
		质料 Material	时期 Period
		铜 Copper	贵霜帝国 Kushan Empire (100-300AD)

035

别外卷 Extra Content Volume	036	题材 Subject Matter 动物 Animal	地域 Region 中亚 Central Asia
		质料 Material 铜 Copper	时期 Period 笈多王朝或后笈多时期 Gupta Empire or Later Gupta Dynasty (300-500AD)

036

别外卷 Extra Content Volume	037	题材 Subject Matter	地域 Region
		神话人物 + 铭文 God & Inscription	南亚 South Asia
		质料 Material	时期 Period
		铜 Copper	笈多王朝或后笈多时期 Gupta Empire or Later Gupta Dynasty (300-500AD)

037

别外卷 Extra Content Volume

038

题材 Subject Matter	地域 Region
动物 + 植物 Animal & Plant	犍陀罗 Gandhara
质料 Material	时期 Period
铜 Copper	贵霜帝国 Kushan Empire (100-300AD)

038

别外卷 Extra Content Volume	039	题材 Subject Matter	地域 Region
		神话人物 God	犍陀罗 Gandhara
		质料 Material	时期 Period
		铜 Copper	贵霜帝国 Kushan Empire (100-300AD)

039

别外卷 Extra Content Volume	040	题材 Subject Matter	地域 Region
		动物（大角鹿） Animal (Megaloceros giganteus)	犍陀罗 Gandhara
		质料 Material	时期 Period
		铜 Copper	贵霜帝国 Kushan Empire (100-300AD)

040

别外卷 Extra Content Volume 041

题材 Subject Matter	地域 Region
动物 Animal	犍陀罗 Gandhara

质料 Material	时期 Period
铜 Copper	贵霜帝国 Kushan Empire (100-300AD)

041

别外卷 Extra Content Volume　　042

题材 Subject Matter	地域 Region
铭文 Inscription	犍陀罗 Gandhara

质料 Material	时期 Period
铜 Copper	笈多王朝或后笈多时期 Gupta Empire or Later Gupta Dynasty (300-600AD)

042

别外卷 Extra Content Volume 043

题材 Subject Matter	地域 Region
铭文 Inscription	犍陀罗 Gandhara
质料 Material	时期 Period
锡合金 Tinalloy	笈多王朝或后笈多时期 Gupta Empire or Later Gupta Dynasty (300-500AD)

043

别外卷 Extra Content Volume 044

题材 Subject Matter	地域 Region
动物（马） Animal (Horse)	南亚 South Asia
质料 Material	时期 Period
铜 Copper	贵霜帝国 Kushan Empire (100-300AD)

别外卷 Extra Content Volume	045	题材 Subject Matter	地域 Region
		动物 + 铭文 Animal & Inscription	南亚 South Asia
		质料 Material	时期 Period
		铜 Copper	贵霜帝国 Kushan Empire (100-300AD)

045

别外卷 Extra Content Volume 046

题材 Subject Matter	地域 Region
动物 + 铭文 Animal & Inscription	南亚 South Asia
质料 Material	时期 Period
铜 Copper	贵霜帝国 Kushan Empire (100-300AD)

046

别外卷 Extra Content Volume 047

题材 Subject Matter	地域 Region
人物 Humankind	中亚 Central Asia
质料 Material	时期 Period
铜 Copper	萨珊王朝 Sasanian Empire (224-651AD)

047

别外卷　Extra Content Volume

048-051

题材 Subject Matter	地域 Region
动物 / 铭文 / 动物 / 动物 Animal / Inscription Animal / Animal	中亚 Central Asia
质料 Material	时期 Period
铜 Copper	萨珊王朝 Sasanian Empire (224-651AD)

048

049

050

051

222

别外卷 Extra Content Volume　　052

题材 Subject Matter	地域 Region
铭文 Inscription	中亚 Central Asia
质料 Material	时期 Period
铜 Copper	700AD

052

别外卷 Extra Content Volume   053

题材 Subject Matter	地域 Region
几何纹 Geometry Pattern	印度北部 Northern India
质料 Material	时期 Period
铜 Copper	1400-1800AD

053

别外卷 Extra Content Volume 054

题材 Subject Matter	地域 Region
铭文 Inscription	西亚或印度西北部 Western Asia or Northwestern India
质料 Material	时期 Period
铜 Copper	伊斯兰时代 The Islamic era 1600-1800AD

054

别外卷 Extra Content Volume

055

题材 Subject Matter	地域 Region
几何纹 Geometry Pattern	中亚 Central Asia
质料 Material	时期 Period
铜 Copper	700AD

055

别外卷 Extra Content Volume   056

题材 Subject Matter	地域 Region
植物 Plant	中亚 Central Asia
质料 Material	时期 Period
铜 Copper	200BC-220AD

056

别外卷 Extra Content Volume 057

题材 Subject Matter	地域 Region
几何纹 Geometry Pattern	中亚 Central Asia
质料 Material	时期 Period
铜 Copper	1000-1100AD

057

别外卷 Extra Content Volume   058

题材 Subject Matter	地域 Region
神话人物 God	中亚 Central Asia
质料 Material	时期 Period
铜 Copper	900-1400AD

058

别外卷 Extra Content Volume　　059

题材 Subject Matter	地域 Region
动物 Animal	印度河谷 Indus Valley
质料 Material	时期 Period
费昂斯 Faience	青铜时代晚期 Late Bronze Age (2000-1500BC)

059

别外卷 Extra Content Volume

060

题材 Subject Matter	地域 Region
植物 Plant	中亚 Central Asia

质料 Material	时期 Period
陶 Clay	铁器时代 Iron Age (500BC-500AD)

060

别外卷 Extra Content Volume   061

题材 Subject Matter	地域 Region
几何纹 Geometry Pattern	中亚 Central Asia
质料 Material	时期 Period
陶 Clay	铁器时代 Iron Age (500BC-500AD)

061

别外卷 Extra Content Volume　　062

题材 Subject Matter	地域 Region
人物 + 铭文（封泥） Humankind & Inscription (Sealed with Mud)	南亚 South Asia
质料 Material	时期 Period
陶 Clay	贵霜帝国 Kushan Empire (100-300AD)

062

别外卷 Extra Content Volume   063

题材 Subject Matter	地域 Region
人物（封泥） Humankind (Sealed with Mud)	南亚 South Asia
质料 Material	时期 Period
陶 Clay	贵霜帝国 Kushan Empire (100-300AD)

063

别外卷 Extra Content Volume　064

题材 Subject Matter	地域 Region
人物 + 铭文（封泥） Humankind & Inscription (Sealed with Mud)	南亚 South Asia
质料 Material	时期 Period
陶 Clay	贵霜帝国 Kushan Empire (100-300AD)

064

别外卷 Extra Content Volume	065	题材 Subject Matter	地域 Region
		人物（封泥） Humankind (Sealed with Mud)	南亚 South Asia
		质料 Material	时期 Period
		陶 Clay	贵霜帝国 Kushan Empire (100-300AD)

065

别外卷 Extra Content Volume 066-074

题材 Subject Matter	地域 Region
几何纹 / 植物 / 铭文 Geometry Pattern / Plant / Inscription	西亚 Western Asia
质料 Material	时期 Period
铜 Copper	希腊化至罗马 Hellenistic Period to Ancient Rome (300BC-500AD)

066

067

068

069

070

071

072

073

074

237

别外卷 Extra Content Volume   075

题材 Subject Matter	地域 Region
铭文（海螺纹） Inscription (Whelk Pattern)	南印度 Southern India
质料 Material	时期 Period
铜 Copper	400-600AD

075

别外卷 Extra Content Volume 076

题材 Subject Matter	地域 Region
人物 (脚掌)+ 铭文 Humankind (Sole) & Inscription	印度北部 Northern India

质料 Material	时期 Period
铜 Copper	1700-1800AD

076

别外卷 Extra Content Volume	077	题材 Subject Matter	地域 Region
		铭文 Inscription	印度北部 Northern India
		质料 Material	时期 Period
		铜 Copper	1700-1800AD

077

别外卷 Extra Content Volume

索引表
INDEX

页码	顺序	总账号	分类号	质料	测量方法	规格 (mm)
174	001	XC11767	YZ5785	绿泥石	直径 × 印章高度	21.42×10.39
175	002	XC11748	YZ5766	绿泥石	直径 × 印章高度	28.16×13.76
176	003	XC11768	YZ5786	绿泥石	长 × 宽 × 印章高度	15.79×6.50×12.36
177	004	XC11754	YZ5772	绿泥石	底 × 高 × 印章高度	16.03×18.05×8.97
178	005	XC11774	YZ5792	绿泥石	底 × 高 × 印章高度	23.52×21.61×10.69
179	006	XC11517	YZ5535	大理石	直径 × 印章高度	23.77×12.78
180	007	XC11665	YZ5683	陶	直径 × 印章高度	24.42×69.27
182	008	XC11775	YZ5793	绿泥石	直径 × 印章高度	15.33×30.05
183	009	XC11777	YZ5795	绿泥石	长 × 宽 × 印章高度	28.85×25.04×10.69
184	010	XC11761	YZ5779	绿泥石	长 × 宽 × 印章高度	17.64×8.59×8.59
185	011	XC11746	YZ5764	费昂斯	长轴 × 短轴 × 印章高度	14.75×11.39×7.38
186	012	XC11753	YZ5771	费昂斯	长轴 × 短轴 × 印章高度	16.81×13.16×8.30
187	013	XC11760	YZ5778	费昂斯	长轴 × 短轴 × 印章高度	18.58×13.57×7.26
188	014	XC11747	YZ5765	绿泥石	长 × 宽 × 印章高度	24.67×18.82×8.31
189	015	XC11762	YZ5780	绿泥石	长 × 宽 × 印章高度	21.88×18.65×10.56
190	016	XC11758	YZ5776	滑石	直径 × 印章高度	9.52×23.77
191	017	XC11755	YZ5773	绿泥石	直径 × 印章高度	26.81×14.17
192	018	XC11876	YZ5894	绿泥石	长 × 宽 × 印章高度	30.14×22.65×8.36
193	019	XC11521	YZ5539	滑石	长 × 宽 × 印章高度	38.85×32.55×14.47
194	020	XC11529	YZ5547	铜	长 × 宽 × 印章高度（3 面）	20.00×8.70×12.30
195	021	XC11784	YZ5802	铜	长 × 宽 × 印章高度（4 面）	12.64×29.82×11.65
196	022	XC11543	YZ5561	铜合金	直径 × 印章高度	23.67×7.86
197	023	XC11281	YZ5299	铜	底 × 高 × 印章高度	18.97×21.78×18.21
198	024	XC11491	YZ5509	铜	长 × 宽 × 印章高度	34.52×32.55×17.02
199	025	XC11311	YZ5329	铜	底 × 高 × 印章高度	27.60×24.59×21.77

续表
CONTINUE THE TABLE

页码	顺序	总账号	分类号	质料	测量方法	规格 (mm)
200	026	XC11535	YZ5553	铜	直径 × 印章高度	18.40×8.82
201	027	XC11446	YZ5464	铜	直径 × 印章高度	25.50×22.65
202	028	XC11779	YZ5797	铜	直径 × 印章高度	16.77×26.36
203	029	XC11309	YZ5327	铜	直径 × 印章高度	26.25×23.99
204	030	XC11302	YZ5320	铜	长 × 宽 × 印章高度	19.17×26.22×5.55
205	031	XC11516	YZ5534	玛瑙	长轴 × 短轴 × 印章高度	16.19×12.63×8.01
206	032	XC11789	YZ5807	铜	长 × 宽 × 印章高度	31.24×20.93×9.92
207	033	XC11544	YZ5562	铜	直径 × 印章高度	19.25×25.76
208	034	XC11798	YZ5816	铜	长 × 宽 × 印章高度	19.31×20.00×16.91
209	035	XC11536	YZ5554	铜	长 × 宽 × 印章高度	20.12×19.64×16.29
210	036	XC11799	YZ5817	铜	直径 × 印章高度	17.56×10.66
211	037	XC11790	YZ5808	铜	长 × 宽 × 印章高度	22.22×22.14×10.15
212	038	XC11793	YZ5811	铜	直径 × 印章高度	33.88×23.90
213	039	XC11537	YZ5555	铜	直径 × 印章高度	20.56×9.31
214	040	XC11540	YZ5558	铜	直径 × 印章高度	22.21×3.64
215	041	XC11786	YZ5804	铜	长轴 × 短轴 × 印章高度	30.91×23.43×7.05
216	042	XC11539	YZ5557	铜	长 × 宽 × 印章高度	21.10×18.36×6.53
217	043	XC11545	YZ5563	锡合金	长 × 宽 × 印章高度	20.00×14.00×8.00
218	044	XC11782	YZ5800	铜	长 × 宽 × 印章高度	15.79×11.66×5.39
219	045	XC11542	YZ5560	铜	直径 × 印章高度	23.26×17.37
220	046	XC11541	YZ5559	铜	长 × 宽 × 印章高度	22.01×22.94×9.25
221	047	XC11794	YZ5812	铜	直径 × 印章高度	19.24×34.50
222	048	XC11533	YZ5551	铜	直径 × 印章高度	13.50×10.42
222	049	XC11531	YZ5549	铜	直径 × 印章高度	11.59×9.35
222	050	XC11532	YZ5550	铜	长 × 宽 × 印章高度	12.54×9.47×12.05
222	051	XC11530	YZ5548	铜	直径 × 印章高度	11.01×8.81
223	052	XC11787	YZ5805	铜	直径 × 印章高度	31.07×10.27
224	053	XC11795	YZ5813	铜	长 × 宽 × 印章高度	36.16×36.06×22.40
225	054	XC11778	YZ5796	铜	长轴 × 短轴 × 印章高度	17.23×11.81×25.88
226	055	XC11791	YZ5809	铜	长轴 × 短轴 × 印章高度	32.28×22.94×11.30
227	056	XC11780	YZ5798	铜	长 × 宽 × 印章高度	26.39×24.09×18.15
228	057	XC11383	YZ5401	铜	直径 × 印章高度	15.40×7.87
229	058	XC11781	YZ5799	铜	长 × 宽 × 印章高度	18.29×11.23×8.62
230	059	XC11526	YZ5544	费昂斯	长 × 宽 × 印章高度	24.00×24.00×20.00

续表
CONTINUE THE TABLE

页码	顺序	总账号	分类号	质料	测量方法	规格 (mm)
231	060	XC11527	YZ5545	陶	直径 × 印章高度	30.00×30.00
232	061	XC11875	YZ5893	陶	长 × 宽 × 印章高度	17.23×13.05×51.03
233	062	XC11524	YZ5542	陶	长轴 × 短轴 × 印章高度	24.03×21.90×13.04
234	063	XC11522	YZ5540	陶	长 × 宽 × 印章高度	23.42×19.10×18.00
235	064	XC11523	YZ5541	陶	长轴 × 短轴 × 印章高度	24.79×21.40×11.03
236	065	XC11525	YZ5543	陶	直径 × 印章高度	38.00×22.00
237	066	XC11866	YZ5884	铜	长 × 宽 × 印章高度	10.96×9.89×21.10
237	067	XC11867	YZ5885	铜	长 × 宽 × 印章高度	11.93×10.83×21.18
237	068	XC11868	YZ5886	铜	长 × 宽 × 印章高度	13.37×10.85×19.09
237	069	XC11869	YZ5887	铜	直径 × 印章高度	11.64×21.14
237	070	XC11870	YZ5888	铜	长 × 宽 × 印章高度	14.67×8.98×20.36
237	071	XC11871	YZ5889	铜	长 × 宽 × 印章高度	12.54×9.21×20.45
237	072	XC11872	YZ5890	铜	长 × 宽 × 印章高度	13.34×10.69×21.63
237	073	XC11873	YZ5891	铜	长 × 宽 × 印章高度	16.34×8.57×22.01
237	074	XC11874	YZ5892	铜	长 × 宽 × 印章高度	11.17×8.69×21.64
238	075	XC11534	YZ5552	铜	长 × 宽 × 印章高度	14.31×14.95×6.54
239	076	XC11785	YZ5803	铜	长 × 宽 × 印章高度	30.70×26.74×21.33
240	077	XC11668	YZ5686	铜	长 × 宽 × 印章高度	23.69×79.28×19.88

后记

原夫文字未萌，图像表意。石陶骨金以征信，古今所同；龙穗鸾体以寄情，中外一契。印迹历史，回响文明。美既善于彼邦，情自钟于我辈。此余所由重域外印章者也。

壬辰春，余偶获域外印章，为之心动神骇，目眩情移。味先民之余烈，挹域外之清芬。遂乃着力购藏，不觉逾纪。刀笔所酬，多尽于此。且迹非一国，印散多方，披沙拣金，去伪存真，所获无多，其难能也极矣。又以其得之也艰，故爱之也弥深。珍逾拱璧，未尝轻以示人。

余素慕前辈贤达高义，每赏馆藏捐赠，辄心向往之。会西泠印社中国印学博物馆有意增设域外印之展陈，与余相商再三。癸卯仲夏，遂以所藏域外印六百余枚，悉数捐赠。馆方授以显要之区，俾资展布。物尽其能，广其流传之意一也。倘能以此为平台，布展研讨，融汇学术，碰撞思想，推动中外印章文化之交流、发展，则古印幸甚，而余亦幸甚。今甄选再三，辑为是谱以为艺林快事。

印谱之行于世者，或宗法先秦两汉，古意斑驳；或取径明清民国，异采纷呈。若余之辑域外印章者，尚未多见也。矧以山川异域，道本同揆。他山之石，可以攻玉。方今信息时代，地球一村，印学之国际交流，方兴未艾。而国内印人，鲜见涉足于此者。余也不敏，愿为抛砖引玉，则是编之所望矣。

印章既捐，余颇幸是印之得所，然意之所钟，拳拳未能忘心者久之，若嫁女然。燕燕之怀既酬，孜孜之求复绍，洵足为平生快事矣。

甲辰清明
何连海于止止山房